DNR

DO NOT RESUSCITATE

**When you face the impossible in life,
but know you'll win no matter the outcome.**

DAVE WALL

TWO PENNY
—— PUBLISHING ——

For permission requests and ordering information, email the publisher at:
info@twopennypublishing.com

Cover photo by: Essie Bergen Artwork

Library of Congress Control Number: 2021913390

ISBN: 978-1-950995-45-5
eBook also available

FIRST EDITION

For more information about Dave Wall or to book him for your next event or media interview, please contact his representative at: info@twopennypublishing.com

| foreword

Every day we read Dave's Facebook posts on Cindy's condition and marveled at his ability to bring us through his words into the situation they faced. But what stood out the most to us was his deeply personal feelings as he watched his wife struggle to live after a brain aneurysm. Sometimes it was so raw and personal, as if Dave had fallen in love with Cindy all over again.

We got the opportunity to visit Dave and Cindy during those first critical days in ICU. Listening to Dave tell the story put us in tears. He was a man who had accepted that his dear wife probably would not recover, and even if she did, her life would never be the same. Yet between the tears and concern, he shared how God had met every need, even the personal ones.

During our visit I mentioned a book I was currently reading titled, "I've Seen the End of You" by Dr. Lee Warren. Just the title of the book alone describes how Dave had felt as he watched Cindy struggle to live. And I believe it helped motivate him to write this book.

We have since had Dave and Cindy over to our place for lunch to hear the whole story. I believe Dave and Cindy's love has grown deeper, not just for each other but for the Lord. Having death come so close peeled a layer of surface away so their hearts are more open, fuller and softer.

This book will remind you that our life is but a vapor and God does not want us to waste any of it, for none of us knows what tomorrow might bring.

Betty Draper

Friend, Blogger, and Missionary with Ethnos360

| prologue

As you begin to read the following account of our lives, my wife, Cindy, and I realize there will be those who agree with our worldview and those who don't. If you don't share our worldview, I'm actually ok with that, and trust as you read our story you will find yourself challenged, humored and coming away thinking there is a lot more to this life than meets the eye.

For those who do share our beliefs, I would simply ask you to come away asking yourself if you really believe what you say you believe. Is your faith real and alive? I wouldn't say your faith has to be ginormous in size and great. It just needs to be mustard-seed size. That's pretty tiny. But it holds the potential of great things if planted in the right soil.

The bottom line is, no matter what you believe, when you are faced with a crisis in your life, your actual beliefs will come to the surface. How much better it is to be prepared, than not.

There is a verse—Philippians 1:21—that reads like this, "For to me, to live is Christ and to die is gain." These few words are very familiar to anyone who has some exposure

> *When you are faced with a crisis in your life, your actual beliefs will **rise** to the surface.*

to the content of the Bible, but whether you have that exposure or not, I would like you to say to yourself the opposite of that verse: "For to me, to live is myself and to die would be a loss." Which way does that verse read best for you? The way it is written in the Bible or the way it may actually be in the living out of your day-to-day life? You see, depending on how you live out that verse will determine how you face life in the good times and the bad times.

Maybe you have experienced the euphoria of success or the depths of despair because of uncontrollable circumstances. As you read this account of the past few months of our lives, ask yourself honestly what your perspective on life is and whether it would determine a gain or a loss.

| day 0
thump

I couldn't remember if I'd been to the bathroom during the middle of the night or not. But now as I rolled over and checked the time, it was 6:00 a.m. and definitely time to drain my not so sizable bladder. I was becoming pretty proud of how long I could hold off making the inevitable morning journey when I knew it wasn't quite time to get up. But ya, it was time to go, so I swung my legs out of bed and to the floor. My eyes told me they were dry and still fought the idea of opening, but I somehow convinced the rest of my 54-year-old body to move. I shuffled through the walk-in closet to the master bathroom and sat. Normally, I would have finished the job and proceeded to the kitchen to put the coffee on for the morning two-cup brew.

But this morning some gears were grinding to life in my brain, and caused me to remember I had a breakfast appointment in town at 8:30 a.m. with a buddy of mine who's a state patrol officer. We originally planned to have breakfast months earlier, but the COVID-19 deal had closed most places for a time. We finally got around to making a new plan to eat at our favorite breakfast place, Raphael's Bakery in downtown Bemidji, Minnesota.

Hmm, maybe I should go back to bed and sleep a little longer, I thought to myself.

Nah, some other thought said. *You can't ever go back to sleep once you get up.*

But the former thought proposal won out, and I returned to bed since I wasn't in a rush anyway.

Cindy was lying on her stomach with her head resting on her left forearm enjoying the peace and quiet with no responsibilities to attend to. Her eyes lazily watched me as I slipped back under the sheets and gave her a little peck of a kiss on her olive-skinned elbow. My eyes closed, and I was back to sleep.

> I finally managed to finger **911** while holding my struggling wife on her side.

I suppose it was 5 to 10 minutes later when I heard the sheets rustle again. It was Cindy's turn to make the morning journey. Still half asleep, she made her way to the other bedroom door leading to the bathroom. I heard a thump.

I thought to myself, *Ha, she mustn't be fully awake and bumped the bedroom door on her way*—something we do regularly when we don't wake up enough to hit the bathroom straight on. I'm not sure why, but I lifted my head and turned to look in her direction. Cindy was lying on the middle of the floor a good six feet from the half-opened door. Thinking she must've had a dizzy spell, I started to move off the end of the bed, but before even stepping to the floor, I could see this was no dizzy spell. Cindy was in full grand mal seizure, frothing at the mouth, limbs twitching, back and neck arching. I dashed to her side, grasping her shoulders.

"Sweetheart, stay with me!" My voice cracked and my eyes teared up.

But then I snapped into emergency mode, relying on training from years on the mission field and working in the sporting and entertainment industry. I rolled her onto her right side to prevent any inevitable vomit from choking her when she came out of the seizure.

"Honey, stay with me. Don't leave me now!" I begged her as I slipped back into husband mode. My eyes teared up again, but I had to make a decision as I trembled while holding my wife.

Cindy and I were not afraid to die. We had lived a life of adventure in the jungles of Papua New Guinea and faced many times of sickness together for both ourselves and our children. But even more than that was our faith in what the Bible teaches about eternal life, it was already settled for us.

My decision was difficult but came quickly, "I'm not going to let you die here. Not here on the bedroom floor," I said aloud.

"You've got to get your phone from the bed stand," the clear command followed out of nowhere. My tears receded as I shot over to the bed, ripping the phone from the charging cord. I returned to my wife, still convulsing, gurgling and gasping for every breath. It seemed like an eternity to scan my finger and get to the keypad in the phone app. I finally managed to finger 911 while holding my struggling wife on her side.

"Beltrami County dispatch, what is your emergency?"

| 30 some years earlier
sylvester

It was a Saturday morning breakfast. I normally didn't get up for breakfast on Saturday mornings. I would rarely get up for a weekday morning breakfast at the small Bible College out on the prairies of Alberta, Canada. But this Saturday morning was different. It was the morning after the first hockey game of the season, and I knew she'd be at breakfast, unlike me... normally. I combed my red locks, threw on some clothes and a jacket, and made my way down to the dining hall with my radar cranked up to high. I burst through the men's entrance with hardly enough time to hang my jacket and in an instant zeroed in on the table where she was sitting.

In those days, the little Bible college had strict dating rules. You couldn't ask a tree out on a date without a summons to the dean's office. But this wasn't a date, technically. It was an opportunity to see how impressed she was about the big game the night before. Besides, it was only a date if you asked the girl out, and I was smart enough not to, and thus skirt around the technicalities.

I don't know if it was bravery, gall, or sheer stupidity, but I sped through the serving line, piled up some whatever-it-was on my plate, and made a beeline to the table where my target sat. Three tables had been joined together with 12 chairs, all but one occupied by pretty young college girls.

It was my lucky day. I didn't ask if I could join the table, a sure sign of the folly of my mission.

It took half a second to sit down, get comfortable and without one bite of food, blurted out, "So what'd ya think of the game last night?"

The screeching sound of the chair sliding back from the table was pleasant compared to the cold words that followed, "I wasn't impressed." And as quickly as I had sat down, Cindy was up and gone about her business for the day.

It was late October, and the sun in Alberta that time of year wasn't strong enough to give you a sunburn, but the remaining 10 gals at the table could see the embarrassed look on my face rivaled any midsummer sunburn. The college didn't normally serve pie at breakfast, but as each of the young ladies left the table, I sat eating my overly large portion of humble pie.

Being stood up in such a grand fashion didn't deter me for long. I licked my wounds and got back in the pursuit game, knowing Cindy was by far the most beautiful woman I had ever seen. The more cold shoulder I got, the more I fell in love. I was completely oblivious to the signs she had no interest in a redheaded punk hockey player who had an ego larger than any of the mountains a short drive to the west of the college. It didn't occur to me she didn't like me and had decided I was the last one in the freshman class she'd ever like.

I kept up the pursuit, as we neared Christmas break, without a care about the dating rules that would fall out of the school handbook when you opened it. I bought Cindy a present for Christmas and talked my sister Donna into delivering it to Cindy's room in no man's land—the women's dorm. The present, a cute little stuffed Sylvester the Putty Tat, got delivered, but it could have fallen into a black hole for all I knew. I never did hear anything about what I thought was a kind gesture.

By the second semester something really weird started happening. I began paying attention in class, taking notes in church and even listening to the teaching. My grades improved and I had a sense God was putting his finger on my heart creating a desire to somehow serve Him. "But Lord, I don't want to be a missionary. This girl I really like wants to be a missionary and no one's ever going to accuse me of doing something for a girl."

Somehow, I sensed a response back, "I guess we'll see about that, won't we."

Through the teaching I sat under on those prairies of western Canada, God continued to soften my heart and bring me to the place of surrender that if he wanted me to give my life in some foreign country for the sake of his kingdom, then I was willing. Little did I know, at that time, I should have fastened my seatbelt, because life took off at breakneck speed.

That spring I was supposed to go on a cross country soccer tour for the college, but I sprained my ankle and had to step off the team. The yearly spring conference was happening at that time, and I hobbled into one of the sessions on crutches only to be greeted by one of the mission reps named Pete. I'm not even sure what prompted me, but I said to the fellow, "I think God wants me to go on a short-term mission trip this summer."

"That's great news, Dave," Pete replied excitedly, reaching in his pocket for his daytimer while directing me into the men's washroom so we could talk. "I'll call down to headquarters right away and get you on a team. Where would you like to go?"

I hadn't thought that through, so I said, "You know, I like this girl and she wants to go to Papua New Guinea so that can't be my first choice. I wouldn't want her or other people to think I'm doing this for a girl."

"Well, then give me a couple of other choices, but we don't have to rule out Papua New Guinea as I know they have teams going there this summer. We can make it your third choice."

"Ok, well how about we try for the Philippines first, Libera second and New Guinea third, just so we give it a chance."

"Perfect," the rep replied, finishing his note. "I'll see you tomorrow and let you know."

The next afternoon, we met again in the exact same location, and before I got close enough, I could see the excitement on Pete's face. He motioned me back into the men's washroom.

"Ok, I got a hold of the folks down at the mission headquarters and here's what they said," he began, barely able to contain himself. "The Philippines is full. Liberia is full. But there's been a cancellation on the Papua New Guinea team!"

"You've got to be kidding," I said slowly with an I-don't-believe-it tone and a half I'm-excited sort of smile. "Ok, I guess if that's what God wants me to do, then that's what I'm going to do." We discussed a few more of the particulars about locking everything in and moving forward with the adventure before heading back out to the auditorium.

I took a seat in the back as the speaker continued his message, but I didn't hear a word. I knew the very next thing I had to do… find Cindy and tell her the great news. Of course, I hoped she'd be impressed and throw me a bone of approval with a nice smile, but I wouldn't push my luck. However, she had to be the first to know. I left the conference meeting knowing exactly where to find her, because I always knew where she was. At this time of day, she would be cleaning in the faculty building as part of her student work on campus.

Thankfully the doors weren't locked yet, so I entered the building making my way down the hall towards the sound of a vacuum. Before I got there, I saw the cord move a little as it stretched across the hall from the outlet. The vacuum shut off. As Cindy came into the hall I hoped she'd be at least a little happy to see me. I saw her surprise, but she quickly recovered.

"Hey," I began in a nervous and almost squeaky voice. "How's it going?"

"Okay, but I am working as you can see," came the quick matter-of-fact reply.

"I have some amazing news," I began as Cindy paid more attention to winding up the vacuum cord on the back of the machine than she did to me. "I'm going to Papua New Guinea this summer."

The winding stopped slightly, giving me a signal of hope I had caught her attention. She looked at me and said, "That's great. I need to keep working." And off she went to the next vacuuming location.

Well, it wasn't a large soup bone size of a response, I thought. *But she did stop what she was doing and actually looked at me. That was worth a chicken bone at least.* I slowly walked backward giving a light wave as if she was still standing there looking at me. I had a choice to make right there and then. Was I going to do this for God? Or for the approval of a girl I was desperately in love with? The former became my resolve, and I pressed on.

My summer in Papua New Guinea turned out to be a life-changing

> *Was I going to do this for God? Or for the approval of a girl I was desperately in love with? The former became my resolve and **I pressed on.***

experience. And what made it even better was Cindy, at the encouragement of her mother, wrote to me the entire time I was gone. Cindy's mom had always wanted to go to the mission field, but had never made it, and therefore told Cindy she ought to write to me—even though I was the worst pick possible in the freshman class.

My sophomore year started with a whole new focus. I became very involved in student life, ministry and was chosen as the captain of the school hockey team. I wasn't intentionally trying to impress Cindy, but I had changed from the year before. I even decided to go on a second summer trip, but this time to Africa.

Halfway through our junior year, I had all but given up on Cindy. I came to the point of realizing she wouldn't ever like me, but one day that all changed. I was sitting in the library working on a paper when someone bumped my elbow while passing by. As I lifted my head to see who it was, I was greeted by the most beautiful and positive smile I had ever seen in my entire life. Cindy had apparently come to the realization that I was growing up and had become serious about my relationship with God. She still had her reservations about me, but decided I was Mr. Right. She had finally warmed up to my persistence and desperate interest in her. Soon after the bump, we began dating as per the rules of the college and never looked back.

After graduating we married, started our family and eventually found our way back to the jungles of Papua New Guinea where we worked for nearly 20 yearsand the whole time, Sylvester the Putty Tat was right there with us.

| three weeks earlier
stuck

Wednesday July 15, 2020

For those who know me well, I am not a carpenter, builder, cabinet maker, or anything close to it. I can't even hang a picture straight. Cindy owns all the power tools in the garage. I'm one of those lucky guys who buys his wife power tools for Christmas and birthday presents. Not only is my wife grateful for these gifts—but she also knows how to use them. It's amazing. Okay, I'll be honest, I still buy hockey and hunting gear, but the balance of the tool gifts helps our marriage function well.

My God-given talents are in language, teaching and working with people. I actually understood how to diagram sentences in high school and college English. Learning a tribal language was a daily adventure for me during our years in Papua New Guinea. I've taught in three languages fluently. Tagmemics, phonemic analysis and translation are tools I know how to use.

Now, in the summer of 2020, I found myself in a job where I needed construction skills. Projects needed to be straight, level, square and above satisfactory to meet the expectations of high-end clients. Those actions are all verbs that are not part of completing sentences in my life. I felt completely inadequate and stressed.

My employment did include something I loved to do—managing a paintball park and a newly-designed challenge course. The latter wasn't quite operational yet. At no fault of my brother-in-law, for whom I worked, I needed to spend more time in construction work because of COVID-19. Revenues were down from the paintball, and the construction provided billable hours and revenue. Therefore, each day I dreaded doing what I wasn't good at. I dreaded the long hours. I dreaded me, because this wasn't me and what I could do best. Nonetheless each day I refused to quit. I needed the shreds of what was left of my honor, and, of course, I needed the income. I felt stuck and couldn't make myself move in any direction.

> Each day I **dreaded** doing what I wasn't good at.

Added to my stress was the plan for the kids to come home and all be together as a family before our son Seth, and his wife Emily, moved to Australia with their two little ones. All 23 of us would be together for the first time. Our son Jordan, his wife Charissa and their kids just moved back to the area the month before, so they were now close by. Our son Chas, and his wife Lexi and their kids were here in Bemidji. Our daughter Essie, and her husband Travis and their two girls were coming from Florida. And our youngest Maea, and her husband Bryan, were close by in Fargo. Cindy and I were beside ourselves with excitement about having all 11 grandkids here. We had to get the "big picture" of all of us at the flagpoles done because who knew the next time we'd all be together again. But I was stressed. Would I get time off while they were here? Would I feel guilty about taking time off? How was it going to work? I wanted time with the family. I decided to just take

Thursday and Friday off no matter what. I wanted the time with my kids and grandkids; I just felt guilty the whole time.

It was wonderful to "sleep in" Thursday and hear the not so little whispers of the grandkids making their way up the stairs in the morning. All donned their cute, little pajamas, bulging in the back with a night's load of what diapers were supposed to hold.

There's nothing better than having a morning brew in your hand and one of the littles crawling into your lap to have a story read by Bubby (our name for grandpa). There was no hurry, as we had the whole day to be together and hang out.

After everyone had breakfast served up, Seth pitched in and began helping Cindy construct her summer project—a chicken coop. The eight chicks she had delivered in mid-June were growing quickly and needed a structure that would house them properly. Cindy had her drawings ready, so she and Seth got busy at construction.

I just enjoyed the day off, playing with the grandkids and making sure their diapers got changed… by their mothers. Because Bubby doesn't do diapers. Ever. It's a family rule. And it's never broken.

On Friday we put a plan in place that as soon as Jordan and his bunch arrived, we'd all gather at the flag poles for the much-anticipated family photo. I was sure to remind everyone at least ten times we had to do the shot right away as there would be no chance of herding all those grandkids back into place if we let them run wild. Texts and phone calls were sent back and forth with ETA's given, hoping to make the plan work. We weren't looking for a studio photo with everyone wearing his/her Sunday best. That wouldn't be the Wall way. No, we just wanted to be ourselves. But of course, it would be ok if the little Wall boys didn't have grass stains or wet pants for the picture.

Jordan and his crew finally arrived, and no sooner were the van doors open than Essie was giving orders for everyone to gather at the flag poles.

"Do the big group photo first before the kiddos realize what is going on," I shouted, hoping to take advantage of the time to make it happen quickly. We somehow managed to get everyone together while Essie set up her camera on a ladder and set the self-timer feature. Not sure how we did it, but with kids squirming like leeches that just had a salt shower, we got the pictures done. All five of our kids, all five spouses and all 11 grandchildren. Now it was pizza time.

We have a pizza oven on our deck that overlooks the beautiful lake we live next to. Each Friday night we try to have family or friends over to enjoy pizza cooked in our Italian Forno as it's called. The difference this night was that it was all of our family together—nothing better. My job was to get the oven fired and hot enough for cooking a ton of pizzas. Inside temp needed to be about 700 degrees Fahrenheit to handle all the delicious cuisine headed its way in short order. I was also in charge of cooking the pizzas. Cindy's job was prepping and rolling out the dough. Tonight's gang was going to need three batches for sure. Cindy also prepped the toppings, but it was sure nice to have Essie and Maea to help, along with the three daughters-in-law.

Inside and outside the house became a beehive of activity with every size and shape of cousin, aunt and uncle running all over to the utter joy and satisfaction of two incredibly grateful grandparents to the whole mob.

The rule for pizza night at the Wall house is that you have to build your own pizza. Doesn't matter the age, old or young, you have to build your own. Our little tradition shocks the many people who come to our place and learn we make our own sauce, dough and then actually build our own pizzas. We hardly ever buy pizza. We always make it from scratch. So, little tots and adults alike got busy with their construction projects and then took them out to Bubby on the deck. I began receiving the pizzas at a rapid rate and could see some were culinary masterpieces and some were akin to those modern art pieces you see in downtown New York, the ones that look like someone just threw paint on the wall. Except I'm pretty sure these art pieces wouldn't stick so well. Nonetheless, all of the artists who presented their work were proud of the job they had done and that was the exact goal we sought to achieve.

With full bellies and diapers, the evening unfolded with storytelling from our days in the jungle and current goals and aspirations for the future. I sat there with my full belly and heart thanking God for my wonderful children, their spouses, and our incredible grandkids. Before I knew it, the Wall clan began to retire for the night. The Littles were equipped with fresh diapers and went off to bed. Adults who had energy to spare, played games until late. Finally, Grammy and Bubby exited the house for the tent trailer friends had allowed us to borrow for extra sleeping room and hit the hay. As I lay replaying the wonderful day and counted saggy diapers like sheep jumping a fence, the last thing I remember was the thrill of getting the big picture done.

Saturday morning came with no responsibilities. *So nice to lie here in the cool of the tent trailer,* I thought to myself. Our nights were cooling off nicely for a mid-July summer in northern Minnesota. Typically, the sticky humidity hung around until morning.

It didn't take long to notice Cindy had already gone into the house. *That's strange,* a lazy thought followed in my mind. *She normally gets up after*

I do. Must have big breakfast plans in mind. I pulled on some clothes and figured I'd head into the house to get the morning coffee going.

I entered the house through the garage and noticed the house was still pretty quiet considering all the inhabitants inside. Essie's girls and Seth's little ones hadn't made it up from their nightly hibernation yet. I fully expected an aroma of cinnamon rolls to greet me at the door. But there was nothing, and Cindy was lying on the couch under a blanket with her head buried in a pillow.

"Are you okay, Hon?" I asked, kneeling beside her, putting my hand on her shoulder.

"Just my head and neck again," came the muddled answer. Several times over the past couple of years Cindy would get the same symptom when she overdid things like raking the yard or using a heavy wheelbarrow.

"Did you take some ibuprofen yet?" I queried not wanting to sound callous, but it usually helped.

"No, not yet," came her weary reply.

"I'll get you a couple," I offered and headed to the bathroom for the medicine and then the kitchen for water.

"Here you go, take these."

Cindy sat up with some effort and took the ibuprofen, then lay back down… for the rest of the day. She threw up a few times later on and, with the help of Essie, tried to keep hydrated accordingly. My thoughts were simply that this round of her neck being out of place was a little worse than before, but she would bounce back tomorrow.

Sunday was no different other than Travis, Essie and the girls moved to the basement so Cindy could sleep in the master bedroom again. No change in my prognosis either. Because Cindy had bounced back from this before, I saw no need for concern.

I was more concerned about returning to work in the morning. I had so enjoyed the time with the kids being home, I dreaded the thought of returning to work I couldn't do.

Although Cindy stayed in bed all day, I kept assuring the kids their mother would be fine; she bounces back for sure by the second day. But then the kids started asking their own questions: "How often would this happen? What would set it off? You didn't have her checked out?" I was a little on the defense stating we rarely went to the doctor unless absolutely necessary. I guess it was the old jungle mentality from years of living in a third world country where you pretty much took care of yourself.

"It's just a little worse this time around," I assured the kids. "Besides, our insurance plan isn't great, and it has a high deductible," I justified.

The rest of the day was spent trying to finish up the chicken coop project knowing Cindy would appreciate it. The chickens were getting too big for the starter coop, but I was really hiding from the uncomfortable place I was in before the kids and their concern for their mother.

Monday still saw no improvement in Cindy's neck pain. She had become lethargic and didn't even want to get out of bed. I knew she wanted to spend every waking moment with the kids, but she couldn't.

I went to another stress-laden day at work. I justified myself by leaving Cindy with the kids. I was checked out as a husband.

Tuesday still saw no improvement, and to my shame, I was completely aloof to what Cindy was going through. We were four days into her sickness, and I was acting as if it was still Saturday morning, thinking she'd get over it like other times. "It's just a little worse this time," I kept saying to myself like someone not realizing the house was on fire and about to burn to the ground. Work took my attention, and I was out the door again.

Close to noon my phone rang, and I could see from the screen it was my sister-in-law Chris. "Hey, Chris," I said in my it's-a-great-day-in-the-neighborhood voice, "What's up?"

"I'm over at the house, and I see Cindy isn't in good shape," she began in an unmistakably concerned voice. "She is lethargic and basically can't get out of bed. I'm taking her to Med-Express to see what's going on and get her some help." I felt the sharp pain of embarrassment stabbing into my pride; my sister-in-law was caring for my wife.

Med-Express is a walk-in clinic that works well for us. There's no ER line up at the door, and they do a pretty good job of diagnosing issues and prescribing treatment. The year before I had developed shingles—another stress induced reaction from my view of work—and Med-Express got me fixed up in good time. I thought I had a bad case of poison ivy.

Cindy saw the doctor, and it was determined she had a kidney infection. Urine samples were collected to be sent away for further culturing and meds were prescribed and started.

Added to my embarrassed pride was the fact Travis and Essie returned to Florida that afternoon. Unfortunately, Essie had to leave seeing her mom like a rag doll, unable to even feed herself. My burden of stress and guilt seemed to be growing by the minute.

Many times in the past I had counseled people that each of us has a "sticky ball" of sorts in our lives. If you don't manage your sticky ball well, more and more items or issues or even non-essential things get stuck to it. Before long, the ball is too heavy to carry, and the weight of it makes life miserable because you are stuck! Well, more and more was being added to my sticky ball, and I wasn't holding up well. There was the issue of work.

There was the issue of the kids coming and the kids leaving. There was the issue of wanting the kids to enjoy their time at home. There was the issue of my wife being sick and not bouncing back like normal. There was the issue of feeling like an idiot and not caring for my wife. The weight was becoming unbearable.

When evening came, I had to do something. My head was heavy and in a fog with seemingly no instruments to navigate the course I was on. I needed relief. I decided to text my brother-in-law and say I wouldn't be back to work until the following Monday because I had to figure out something for Cindy. The decision gave me a little breathing room for the time.

Cindy and I are not big medicine people. We try to stay away from prescription meds as much as possible. Ibuprofen is about the extent of what's in our bathroom cabinet, and we rarely used it at all. We aren't anti-medication, but we'd much rather live a healthy lifestyle and do without a medicine cabinet full of pills.

Several years ago, I had the septic tank pumped and the fellow doing the job commented, "You guys don't use any meds, do you?"

I nearly swallowed my dentures (and I don't even have any) shocked he'd ask such a question, but then figured if he was pumping septic tanks, he probably wasn't up on the current HIPAA laws. "Why do you say that?" I queried back with a slight smile on my face.

"Because your tank is super easy to pump," he declared, sliding the large hose back down into the grass covered tank. "I've been to some places where you can hardly suck a drop out of the tank because all the bacteria needed to break things down is dead, killed by all the meds getting flushed down with the... well you know what." The fellow moved back to the truck and began working the controls.

"Never would've thought of that before," I replied with a tilt of my head and shrug of my shoulders. "I guess this guy is a little more than first meets the eye," I didn't say aloud.

So, we aren't big on meds.

But on the other side, we aren't big on homeopathic medicine either. Outside of eating healthy, exercising, and taking care of ourselves, we don't do a lot of herbal supplements, vitamins, or essential oils. We have family and friends who use them, and we are okay with that, but we are just kind of in the middle with everything. But now with a sick wife going on her fifth day of not getting out of bed, I was pretty much willing to try anything!

On Wednesday our daughter-in-law Lexi arranged for a visit to a chiropractor/naturopath doctor in another town about an hour and a half south. I wasn't skeptical at all because of the situation at hand; I just wanted to help Cindy.

The drive was uneventful and Cindy slept stretched out in the back seat of the car. I kept pushing for her to drink lots of fluid as we moved along for the hour and a half trip.

After a wait in the parking lot of the clinic, we were finally able to see the doctor. I helped Cindy out of the car and walked her into the building toward the appropriate exam room. There was no concern for wearing masks even though there was in many other public places because of COVID-19. The clinic smelled amazingly fresh and it had a noticeably friendly atmosphere. I felt a tinge of confidence as we waited for the doctor in the neat and tidy exam room with Lexi, our daughter-in-law.

Before long the door of the room creaked on its hinges and in came a young, clean-cut chiropractor. The doctor had an amazing bedside manner, and immediately Cindy felt comfortable, even though she had zero energy left in her reserve.

"What can we do for you today?" He asked Cindy in a polite voice.

"Well," Cindy began mustering some strength to begin talking, "I've been pretty much unable to get out of bed the last number of days."

I could see Cindy didn't have the fortitude to explain all that had happened, so I took over and chronicled the past number of days beginning with last Friday's pizza party and family reunion. I covered some history with neck aches, the visit and diagnosis from MedExpress and then the option of this visit to see if anything else could be done as this round of not feeling well had gone on too long.

The chiropractor listened well and took notes for each point of the recent history. "Ok, I'm going to go ahead and do some testing right here in the exam room and let your body tell me what the problem is." He began going through each part of the body verbally, looking for reactions. At the end of the session, I wasn't sure what to think, but the conclusion from the doctor was she was suffering from kidney stones.

Hmmm, I thought to myself. *That does somewhat align with the MedExpress diagnosis of a kidney infection.* I tried not to reveal anything while assessing things in my own mind, but the puzzle pieces of Cindy's condition weren't fitting together for me. If it was a kidney infection that was caused by kidney stones, shouldn't she have some acute pain in her lower back? Cindy had some discomfort in her lower back, but the pain was more in the neck area. I decided to just go along with what the doctor was saying, because at this point, I just wanted help for my dear wife any way I could get it.

We left the clinic with an assortment of different probiotics and a cleanser for the digestive system that would help break down the kidney stones. I was marginally optimistic, but again, I just wanted help.

During our time away to see the naturopath doctor, our five kids (Essie called in from Florida) had been talking about the condition their mother was in, and they felt they needed to sit down with me, their dad, and have a heart-to-heart discussion. You know, when you raise your kids in a loving home with all the support they need to make it in life, it tends to come full circle. The plan was to have the boys talk with me later that evening and address a few things with me.

When Cindy and I got home and had some supper, I noticed Chas and Jordan arrived at the house and began talking with Seth. The three brothers appeared to be discussing something serious when they made their way into the house and asked if I would join them on the pontoon down at the lake. I really had no idea what was going on, so I agreed to head down to the lake with them for whatever reason they had in mind.

It was a beautiful still evening with loons calling back and forth to each other. We made our way down our grassy slope in the front yard to the floating dock, a project of Cindy's she'd completed a few years back. The dock creaked with the weight of us making our way down to the pontoon moored at the end in the open water. A couple of startled ducks shot up out of the reeds, quacking their alarm at our sudden arrival. The intention of the time I soon found out wasn't to go for a pontoon ride, it was to sit down with dad and share their hearts. The peace of the still lake water set a perfect stage of peace for our time together—the setting each of the boys was hoping for.

We each took a seat on the pontoon when Seth, our youngest son, began our visit with something I'm sure was quite difficult for him, being the shyest of our kids. "Dad," he began without the slightest trace of a quiver in his voice. "Over this past week, we have become very concerned about you. Yes, mom is sick and that concerns us as she doesn't seem to be improving at all, that goes without saying. But we are concerned about you because you seem to be completely aloof and checked out. Your heart and mind aren't even here. You raised us all to be godly men and take the responsibility of loving our wives and families seriously. You raised us to be faithful in the tasks we took on while growing up." He paused for a bit letting his words sink in. "But now, we are watching you, and you aren't even here in your heart and mind. Mom can't even get out of bed, and it's like you are far away on another planet. It's like you don't even care," he laid out clearly and graciously. "Dad, where are you?" he asked as I sat there like a hollow mannequin. "You are not an example I even want my kids to see right now."

I couldn't respond to what I just heard. I'm not sure if it was the shock of what was said or the shock of who said it, but a vacuum had been created in my heart and mind that prevented me from opening my mouth with a response.

Seth's words cut to my heart. They were wounds I wanted to react to with some sort of defense. But I couldn't. They were the truth. As Seth talked, I realized what a man he had become. He was so brave to sit his father down and confront him with what needed to be said. His skill in handling me was not meant to be lethal even though it hurt. Each of his penetrating words was spoken in love, kindness and grace. And even though each word was hard to receive, each one was meant to get my attention—not to destroy me, but to restore me. In the same way I handled him and each of his siblings in discipline when they were younger, Seth was now modeling that discipline with me. I sought to be faithful with my children when they were growing up in order to prepare them to be faithful in life. Sometimes that meant discipline would hurt so it would get their attention in their disobedience. But the pain wasn't meant to destroy, it was meant to restore. Now, my faithful son sought to get the attention of his father and restore him to his responsibility of loving his wife who needed him.

As I stared at the floor of the pontoon kicking at a piece of imaginary grass in the field of my thoughts, Jordan, our most sensitive and compassionate child, took his turn.

"Dad, you know we love you. We have a great amount of respect for you because of the way you raised and equipped us for our own journeys in life," he began in such a loving and tender manner. "But I have to agree with Seth, you're not even here when Mom needs you most. Each of us is learning to care for our wives, and we know we aren't perfect. But Dad, you seem to be completely checked out, and we want to know what is bothering you," he concluded.

I had no question the boys knew what was bothering me, but they wanted me to agree with them, just as I had worked with them in their younger years. Confession is good for the soul. When God asked Adam in the garden, "Where are you?" and "Who told you, you were naked?" God knew the answers. But he allowed Adam the opportunity to agree with him about his sin. Now, as with Adam, I was being given an opportunity to agree with my sons about what was troubling me.

Chas, our figure-it-out and fix-it child, took his turn, and with tears in his eyes continued, "Dad, I can't bear to see Mom sick like this. She can't even get out of bed because she's so weak. But even more than that, I can't bear to see your apparent lack of concern for her. You keep saying she'll get over it, but we don't see that. And that's why we're setting this time aside to ask you what is wrong. What is bothering you? Why are you so checked out?"

I could feel my heart sinking inside my chest. I hung my head and began weeping in shame. Had I really come to the point where my sons had to do the hard yards with their dad and confront him as they were?

"I feel like such a failure, guys," I began without looking up from my imaginary field. "Every day I go to work feeling like such a loser. I don't have the skills to be a builder as each of you knows so well. I didn't realize I would be doing so much construction, and I'm just completely stressed out. It's like I'm stuck. I don't want to quit and let your uncle down, but at the same time, I resent every day I have to be the guy that can't make anything straight or perfect or acceptable. I just don't know what to do. I need the income, but I'll be honest, I'm consumed with stress about my work."

Chas was quick to jump in. "Dad, you are not a failure," he reassured me. "Look at what you've done in your life. You learn language like none other, and you are so good at working with people. You've been an amazing example to us, your kids. You've directed each one of us to a relationship with God, and we are forever grateful for that."

I looked up from the pontoon floor and met the loving eyes of three of the best men I know on the planet. They weren't looking at me in condemnation or scorn. The support flowing out of them for me was tangible and strong, holding me close to them after the hard words they had just applied to me.

"Dad, we want you to know that we would suggest you quit your job,"

Chas continued as he laid out some direction on behalf of the other two. "We'll support you for as long as we need to until you find work that suits your gifts and abilities. Take the time to be with mom and be alongside her, she needs you 24/7 right now."

I had always taught the kids not to be quitters. I always had them, as they were growing up, finish what they started out to do, because in life they would need that skill when they faced challenges in work and marriage and raising their own families. But now they were suggesting I quit? Did I really hear what was just said? My head swirled in confusion. Did my kids just give me a way out of my situation?

And then it became clear to me…they didn't want me to quit on my wife. They were more concerned about my being the husband I ought to be than sticking at a job. They were more concerned about their mother than my showing up at work again. They were more concerned I was in a job that fit my gifts and abilities. Suddenly I felt a burden lifted off me. Suddenly I was leaving the field I had felt stuck in the middle of for what seemed like forever.

I thought back to an illustration a dear friend of mine would use about leadership. Back in the old west, a sheriff would have certain men he could count on in the tough times. The men were called Hat Men. The Hat Men would come to surround and support the sheriff when it was needed most. Well, this old sheriff was plodding along on his horse with his head down and discouraged. But suddenly, his Hat Men rode up alongside him to give him support and help him get back on the trail and stay in the saddle.

| two weeks earlier
ER

Thursday July 23, 2020

Cindy was 48 hours into her antibiotics and there was still no measurable improvement in her condition. She lay on the couch like someone who had been sick her whole life. No strength, no energy and no appetite. I decided it was time to take her to the ER.

I walked her to the car and had her lie down in the back seat for the 15-minute drive into town. Who cared about seat belts at this point, I just wanted help for my wife.

We checked in at the ER, and thankfully it wasn't too busy, so we managed to get into an exam room and see a doctor right away. We went through the history of the last week making sure the doctor understood Cindy was about 48 hours into her antibiotics for what we believed to be a kidney infection. The bedside manner of the doctor was pleasant, and I believe he wanted to help Cindy get to the bottom of her ailment. After our short discussion, he exited the room and we waited. And waited. And waited. I had a beard at the time, but I was pretty sure I could have grown a new one in the time it took for someone to show up again.

Finally, the door opened again and in came a jovial nurse who was on the tail end of her nursing career or so it looked to me. She rolled in a cart with a tray on it about the size of a football field lined with about as many items as two football teams. The happy nurse began removing packaging from the items and rearranging them on the tray, and that's when I got a little nervous, "So what is all that for?"

Thankfully our friendly nurse was more than willing to explain the layout to me. She began her dissertation, "This is a shot for nausea. This is a shot for pain. This is a…"

"Wait, wait, wait," I cut off the nurse. I wasn't quite as loud as our local fireworks on the Fourth of July, but I was pretty taken back at today's lineup waiting for the down, set, hut-hut! "She doesn't have any nausea," I told the nurse in plain Canadian English.

"Oh," came the response, "then we won't give her that."

"And she's not in pain either," I continued.

"Oh, then we won't give her that shot either."

I was trying to fathom what just happened. Why on God's green earth were they going to give Cindy those shots when clearly she didn't have symptoms for them? Anyway, the nurse went on to explain she needed to draw blood for labs and also hook up some saline for rehydration. Ok, I could handle that.

The nurse proceeded to fill several vials with Cindy's blood samples and then happily left the room just as she had entered. I might have missed the click of the heels on the way out but wouldn't doubt if it happened. She was such a happy nurse.

Cindy fell asleep immediately.

Then we waited. And waited. And waited. By the time I was imagining my third beard of the day, the door opened, and the doctor returned, waking Cindy from her lengthy yet enjoyable nap. "We've done all the labs except for tick-borne tests, the results of which will come back in two days. All other tests came back negative. Your potassium is a touch low, but nothing to worry about. There is no sign of infection in either the urine or kidneys at this point which would concur with your normal temperature. We'll see what the tick analysis shows on the weekend, but until then, stay hydrated and mitigate any pain with ibuprofen as needed. If you have any issues over the weekend, don't hesitate to call the ER and have them direct you to me." And with that, the doctor concluded we were free to go.

*My **thoughts** were being bounced around like a small child in a bouncy house commandeered by thoughtless teenagers.*

But I wasn't free in my mind. In a matter of three days, we had three opinions: kidney infection, kidney stones and negative lab work. I wasn't sure what to think other than Cindy was not getting better.

Friday still brought no change. Cindy was still weak and unable to get out of bed. To say I was concerned would be an understatement. No medical facility of any kind was giving us answers.

Seth, Emily and their two kids left for Australia from Bemidji just after lunch. Before leaving they gathered around Cindy's bedside and prayed for healing and restoration of health. I felt so bad again. Another one of my children was leaving their mother in a terrible state. But they had international connections to make and therefore headed to their new home in Tasmania.

Saturday began again with no measurable change. I went to town to run a few errands and pick up some groceries. MedExpress called with the results of their extended urinary culture and indicated Cindy had a urinary tract infection (UTI) not a kidney infection. They sent over a new prescription to Walmart and changed her medication from Bactrim to Ciprofloxacin. It worked perfectly to pick up the meds as I was already in town.

My thoughts were being bounced around like a small child in a bouncy house commandeered by thoughtless teenagers launching me in the air and laughing each time I landed out of control. I didn't know what to think; had a kidney infection diagnosis, a kidney stone diagnosis, a battery of lab work that turned up nothing and now a UTI diagnosis. What in the world do we do? Oh, and I quickly called the ER again to get the results for the tick-borne tests—all negative.

I headed home as fast as I could. We had used Cipro/Keflex overseas many times, so we were familiar with the antibiotic. Finally, I had a small measure of confidence we were going to get Cindy through this. It had gone on far too long. Not even malaria would last this long for us back in the jungles of Papua New Guinea. Three to four days was max with a bout of that. As I was driving home, I thought back to the time when Cindy was pregnant with Seth, and she had a really bad run of malaria. She was so sick she wasn't able to keep anything down, so in consultation with our doctor over the radio, I gave her injectable quinine in the buttocks. We had learned to give injections, suture (many tribal people and all five kids), pull teeth and various other medical procedures where there was no doctor, but us. Just an aside, but when you give an injection to a tribal person you must be extra careful…not to bend the needle. Their skin is nearly as tough as the rawhide treats you give your dog.

I prepped Cindy for the injection, thankful her skin wasn't rawhide tough. The quinine was super thick, and it took some force on my part to inject it. Cindy winced in pain, so I knew it must've really hurt even with her incredible pain tolerance. I accomplished the task, withdrew the needle and felt a sense of relief that we'd get my dear pregnant wife through this round of the nasty tropical parasite. But my relief was cut short when Cindy lifted her head and looked at me with daggers in her eyes, "Don't ever do that again." Cindy recovered shortly thereafter, and when Seth was born, we noticed he had several cowlicks on his little blond head. We just chalked it up to that bought of malaria while "in the oven" and the nasty quinine shot that saw him through.

I arrived at the house cautiously excited to get Cindy going on the Cipro but was faced with another diagnosis and treatment to consider. While I was gone, Chas had taken a hair sample of Cindy's down to the cities for some testing. I wasn't sure what to think of the whole idea, but I was willing to look at anything that provided some hope. The hair sample came back with confirmation of the UTI and non-respiratory COVID-19.

"Whaaaa?" I said so loud the neighbors could've heard! "This is getting ridiculous." My head was spinning with all the diagnoses on the table. The diagnosis came with a short naturopath treatment which I agreed to have Cindy do, but the next day I would go with what I knew and was familiar with and begin Cindy on the Cipro.

Sunday came and Cindy wasn't in any shape to head to church. Besides, with the whole COVID-19 thing we weren't wanting to go to church in a mask, unable to shake hands and sit six feet apart. Call us rebels if you like, but we had been doing "home church" with friends and family since March anyway. But today, we weren't even going to do that. Cindy was just not well enough, so we stayed home and took advantage of the time to rest.

By midafternoon Cindy got up after sleeping soundly all morning on the couch. "I actually feel a little bit of energy today," she commented with a tinge of caution in her voice.

"Well, that's the best news I have heard in over a week," I supported. "Today, we'll get you going on the Cipro and finish this whatever it is off for good," I was only too happy to add. Finally, some light at the end of the tunnel.

I made a late lunch and Cindy returned to the couch for another nap. While cleaning up it was good to finally have a glimmer of hope shining in the direction of recovery. The only thought I had still dragging behind me was not knowing what the ailment was. The UTI seemed to make sense, because there were a few symptoms that fell in line with it, like short-term memory issues. That had shown up a few times in the last week. But there was one other thing I noticed mid-week that was hanging out there too. One morning Cindy's pupils were dilated in a strange way. I searched my mind for days for words to describe them; they were large and almost wild. The edges weren't defined but looked like a dab of watercolor paint when you dropped some on a sheet of paper and the edges dissipated. The pupils caught my eye, but I had kept the observation to myself.

Cindy continued to sleep a lot on Monday, but she was noticing a little more energy than the day before. I continued to be uncertain about all the diagnoses we had received, but now that we were seeing an increase in energy, I was even more uncertain as to what was helping her. Was it kidney meds, UTI meds, natural remedies, rest, or did whatever it was run itself out? It would have been nice to know what she had been through, but at this point, all I cared about was her feeling better.

We decided with the input of some family and friends to visit the chiropractor again and see if there was any other advice we could get to continue to help Cindy. So we headed down the road to visit the clinic again.

Cindy wasn't excited about the trip as she didn't have the energy for traveling in the car for what would amount to about five hours in all. But she was wanting help and that won out over her desire to just stay home and sleep.

The first time we visited the clinic, they didn't align Cindy's back and neck, as they felt it was fine. But this time I hoped they would do so and provide some needed comfort for her.

We got to the clinic and didn't have to wait to see the doctor. We got the older of the chiropractors and hoped we'd get a second opinion on Cindy's situation.

"Cindy, tell me what's going on today," the doctor asked after explaining his desire to have Cindy's body tell us what was wrong. Cindy went on to explain the past week and a half as best she could. After listening the doctor began by massaging Cindy's feet. I could tell he was pressing pretty hard on certain points of her feet as Cindy did some wincing as he moved about from pressure point to pressure point. Each time, the doctor asked how she was feeling. She would respond without a lot of commitment so then the doctor started putting droplets of various liquids under her tongue as he moved through the exam. One of the droplets was Quinine! That was a shock. Oral quinine is the worst tasting stuff on the planet. The doctor proceeded to crack Cindy's neck in hopes of relieving some of the discomfort she was experiencing.

All in all, the visit was fine, but we weren't sure we came away knowing anything new. The doctor still felt Cindy was suffering from kidney stones. We left with another battery of drops and probiotics to continue taking along with the Cipro prescribed by MedExpress.

That evening, after getting home, I knew it was time to head down the laneway to visit my brother-in-law and give him the news I needed to step away from work. I prepared my mental notes and shot him a text to let him know I'd like to come by when he got home from work.

The time with my in-laws went okay, as I sat at the counter explaining my thoughts. For me it wasn't Cindy's health that was the underlying issue; it was a symptom of the underlying issue. I needed to step away because I was trying to do a job I didn't want to do and, even more importantly, I couldn't do. So, I quit and entered the official world of being unemployed at 54 years of age with a wife who was sick and not recovering well.

The slow walk back to my house was weird. I felt shame for being a quitter. But I also felt relief and freedom with each step that took me closer to our modest lake home. My thoughts went back to the pontoon time with the boys. It felt right to listen to their correction, take it to heart and obey their advice. How bizarre is that? Role reversal of the parent-child relationship like I had never seen before but was thankful to experience. That night I slept well. I was in a position that only God himself could fix.

The next morning I took my time getting out of bed, or in other words, it was 6:00 a.m. and I put the coffee on. Normally, the coffee was hot in the pot as I would have set it up the night before to be ready when I got up. But now that I was "retired" I wasn't sure what time I would start the day, so I didn't set it up. It's funny how you need an alarm to wake you up for work, but then when you don't have work, you wake up automatically at the same time anyway.

I left Cindy sleeping peacefully and began the day like any other normal day. But it wasn't a normal day—I wasn't going to work. I wasn't sure how to feel. Enjoy the freedom to relax and care for my wife? Or carry a cloud of guilt from the visit down the laneway the night before.

I poured my first cup of unemployment coffee and stood overlooking the lake that had greeted me each morning for the past 10 years. It didn't matter the day, whether stormy, sunny, or frozen in the middle of winter, the lake always greeted me with joy, hope and peace. "Lord you have proven yourself faithful over and over again my whole life," I began in conversation. "But why is it that in each new trial it's like my faith tank is completely empty again? I feel like a child taking his first steps again. I don't have the energy to do this anymore. I should be nearing retirement for real, not unemployment. But here I am once again in a place only you can take care of."

As I stared out over the lake sipping on my morning cup of joe, I remembered back a few winters when ice covered the lake. It was frozen. Stuck just like I was. At night you could hear the lake eerily moaning as the temperature of the water underneath wrestled with the air above in a show of strength of who would be in control. The phenomenon of physics is amazing to listen to and sounds like a conversation between moaning giants. The intimidating chorus causes you to fear taking even one step out onto the surface, but the truth is the ice is thick and safe. If the ice were thin, you wouldn't hear anything, and it would be too dangerous and risky to venture out on. When you come to understand the sounds of thick, solid ice, it becomes a peaceful and beautiful symphony telling you it is safe to walk upon. This particular morning I thought back on, was memorable because when I awoke there was a perfectly formed cross on the lake that somehow appeared during the night. And it reminded me that, even though at times it feels like the whole lake is going to break apart at the thunderous sounds of the ice expanding and contracting, God is still in control of everything that is going on.

My unemployment brew needed a refill. As I turned from the beautiful view of the lake, God had already refilled my cup, and I knew he was going to take care of us once again. The sounds of my groaning heart would again turn into a beautiful chorus of God's faithfulness, somehow and some way that only He could do.

Cindy was about the same. Still not much energy. Still sleeping a lot.

| one week earlier
unhandyman

Thursday July 30, 2020

I awoke to another day of only one responsibility: spend time with my dear wife. While I was enjoying my morning coffee again, an email popped up on my phone from my sister-in-law down the laneway. "Thought of you this AM," it read and attached was a screenshot of a county administration position looking to hire. The gesture was thoughtful of her, and I appreciated her understanding my desire to find work that better suited my abilities. Truth be told though, I had applied for a different administration position with the county earlier in July. I just hadn't told anybody because of the circumstances of still being employed by my brother-in-law at the time. Nonetheless, I took the time before the start of the day, which had nothing to start, and filled out the online application.

My day actually did have a plan. I wanted to put the finishing touches on Cindy's chicken coop, so, ironically enough, I was doing what I didn't love to do—carpentry. But this was a chicken coop, not a million-dollar home. Nothing had to be perfectly square. I found myself relaxed working away similar to the days back in the tribe when I'd work all week perfecting my ability in language acquisition and then play bush carpenter on the weekend. Out in the jungle, nobody had to see my carpentry skills or lack of them. The tribal people didn't care about my building inexpertise; they were happy to just have us there living among them. No concern about how square things turned out, just thrilled I was taking time to learn how to communicate with them in their language. The weekends in the tribe gave me a chance to "relax" by finishing projects around the house to make our jungle home livable, mostly.

Nope, the chickens only cared about the amount of feed inside the coop. And for me, their lack of expectation of a perfect home put me at ease, and I felt relaxed tinkering away at making it livable, mostly.

Inside the coop I was busy caulking the seams between the sheets of chipboard paneling, getting it ready for winter. The insulation was all in and I was feeling a sense of accomplishment at how the project was coming along. I stepped outside to grab another tube of caulking and was completely startled to see Cindy standing right there. "Honey!" I nearly yelled. "You scared the chicken liver and other stuff right out of me! What are you doing?"

"I just thought I'd come out to see your fine carpentry skills," she said with a lovely, cornered smile. "Would you mind getting me my grandpa's old yard chair so I can watch and be your audience of one?"

I chuckled with a large heap of doubt sprinkled on my response, "It's not much of a show, and you'll have to join my audience of chickens. They think I'm doing a great job!"

"You always do a great job, honey," Cindy stated with all sincerity drawn from the deep well of love for her inept husband. "And I know the chickens really appreciate all the effort you are putting into this project for them."

Ha! I thought to myself as I turned to fetch her a chair. *I need to have a talk with her about how to lie without the other person knowing.*

"And I appreciate your efforts too, because there's no way I have the energy to get it done myself," she concluded as I returned with the old red garden chair that belonged to her grandpa Verlund.

"You must be feeling a bit better venturing out this far today," I said, stating the obvious with a touch of hope in my voice.

"I do feel a little better," she countered looking up at me as she sat. "And not wanting to miss this show gave me the motivation to get out here." My subsequent eye-roll needed no words to communicate its obvious meaning.

Friday began slowly again. No rush and no auto-start set on the coffee maker, but as per normal I was up about 6:00 a.m. and threw the coffee on for my two-cup morning ritual. I checked through the vitals on my phone: bank and credit card accounts, email, news, Instagram and then finally Facebook as I sipped on a cup of Dunkin's. For years I'd awakened to Tim Horton's coffee out of Canada, but the US stores had some falling out with corporate and closed them all. Sad day, but Dunkin's wasn't a bad way to start the day either.

With coffee in hand, I shuffled outside and made my way out to the new ritual, letting the chickens out. Each morning the layers looked forward to my arrival as I would call them on my approach to their coop. Each one of the girls was big enough to make her way out of the coop and free-range around the property eating grass and catching bugs. Watching their antics was therapeutic in a way, and I had the whole day to benefit from their silly ways.

I headed back inside the house to grab a bit of breakfast before setting out to conquer the day's agenda: attaching the laying box to the side of the coop where the hens would conveniently place their eggs for our benefit. Not an easy task for Mr. Ten Thumbs to accomplish but somehow it needed to end up straight and square.

Cindy was in no hurry to get up, so I set out to do the impossible again, but thankfully without the pressure of a money-paying client—just a little flock of delightful hens that clucked in appreciation when I would feed them each day. They didn't care what their abode looked like, and the only contract fulfillment they required was an unending supply of feed they could peck at.

The laying box began to take shape, and I managed to get it done in a decent fashion. I didn't throw the level on it, but it looked straight, at least compared to the trees standing in the background. Pretty sure the rustling of their leaves was their chuckling at my pathetic skills in carpentry.

I stood admiring my lack of skills when I was startled back to earth by a quiet voice, "It looks wonderful, honey."

"You are so sneaky quiet!" I said in a burst of surprise like a confetti cannon. "You're getting as quiet as a bear coming out here as I'm working."

"Well, you were on another planet in another solar system admiring your work," she quipped. "Being that far away you wouldn't be able to hear a thing."

I chuckled, turning my head back to my masterpiece of a coop, which was a little better looking than the modern art decorating the street corners in town. "Yeah, being that far away you can't see my mistakes either," I began. "Don't look too closely. Stay a couple of light years back while observing."

"Honey," Cindy began with empathy and understanding in her voice knowing I needed it, "It looks wonderful, and the chickens will be proud to call it their home."

"I appreciate the encouragement," I began in a falling tone. "But chickens don't talk or care about what they live in."

"Yeah, but they look pretty happy to me, and I'm happy too," Cindy assured me as we had our first hug of the day.

As the day went on, I could sense I was relaxing and beginning to enjoy life a little more. Sure, I didn't have work and my wife wasn't in the best of health, but my heart and mind were at rest.

Cindy was showing signs of feeling better with more energy and strength. We discussed going out for a boat ride, and she seemed up for the idea. A good sign for sure.

Saturday was yardwork day, so soon after breakfast, I got busy trimming around the yard and dock with the gas-powered trimmer. Cindy is always after me about how much grass there is to mow, but I don't mind. There's just something relaxing about taking care of a big yard. Must be a guy thing, but I like lots of grass, and I always make sure the edges are not overrun by the growth of the trees and bush surrounding us. Each week I would change the mowing pattern and mow a different direction for the health of the grass and to avoid causing ruts in the lawn. This week was an angled cut, and I was ever careful to make sure the lines were as straight as possible. I knew Seth would be watching from Australia; he's the master of perfectly straight lines when it comes to mowing. Oftentimes I would text him a picture to show him how well I was doing with all he taught me about mowing to perfection. Kind of silly I know, but it was an inside joke between us for years.

Later in the afternoon when the yard was looking nice and trim again, Cindy and I decided to head out on the lake. I made my way down to the dock and fired up the boat in preparation for our excursion. The boat had a fair bit of water in it from a few nights of rain the past week, and I figured I'd better bail it out before Cindy boarded. Instead of bailing the water with a bucket, I traversed the channel from the dock through the thick midsummer stands of wild rice to the open water. I'd learned many years before living in the South Pacific it was much easier to drain the boat out than bail it out.

So, once out on the open water, I pulled the drain plug and did a few laps in a circular pattern until all the water had exited. The whole time I was doing this I was looking back toward the dock to see if Cindy had come down waiting for me to pick her up. But she didn't come. I thought that was odd as she seemed pretty excited to go for a ride.

With the water all drained out, I decided to head back to the dock. Still no Cindy. I moored the craft and headed up the hill to the house. "Hey, honey," I called once inside. "Are you here?"

A soft reply came back, "Yes, I'm here."

"How come you didn't come down to the dock? I was looking for you the whole time," I stated as gently as I could.

"I was down there waving my arms trying to get your attention, but I guess you couldn't see me."

"Really?" I was immediately smitten with guilt. I thought for sure I would've been able to see her while draining the boat. *Had I really missed her?* I thought to myself.

"Well, there's still time. Let's head down there and go for a ride," I mustered with renewed enthusiasm that I hoped would help Cindy's disappointment.

"No, it's okay. I really don't have the energy to go down there again," she affirmed. "We can go another day."

"Ughhh," I said to myself, slumping my shoulders and feeling like a failure again. I felt like such a jerk. I should've just come right back to the dock.

Sunday we still weren't ready to venture back to church, but Cindy was showing marked improvement in energy and strength. It was her last day of Ciprofloxacin and we were hopeful she was done with being sick and could get back to normal. In a few short weeks, she would be watching the grandkids again with the return of Lexi, our daughter-in-law, back to her teaching position at the high school. With the whole COVID-19 pandemic and the closing of school back in March, grandma was more than ready to have the littles again each weekday.

It's impossible to write in words how much Cindy enjoys her time watching those kiddos. And Chas and Lexi loved having Cindy watch the kids knowing each day they were cared for in a wholesome way that included lots of love and attention. The treasure box was the favorite part of each day for both Cindy and the kids. When the kids arrived at the house each morning, Cindy had a little box that contained a surprise linked to the day's Bible story. It was such a creative and fun way to teach the kids, and Cindy considered it a huge honor to have that opportunity with the littles.

Cindy got up with me on Monday morning for the first time in over two weeks. She was definitely showing signs of getting better. I made her the customary over-easy egg and toast for breakfast, and we sat at the table with the morning view of the lake as our company. I felt a sense of relief spending the time with her and had hopes of life returning to normal again.

"I'm so glad to see you up and about, honey," I began, taking a sip of coffee.

"Yeah, I feel much better today. I guess the Cipro did its job and I'm finally over that UTI. Weird how it lasted so long," she observed while dipping the crust of my homemade bread into the golden yolk of her egg. "How long has it been anyway?" She asked, looking at me with a crinkled brow. "Two weeks?"

"Actually, two weeks ago Saturday. We've had quite the time trying to figure out what the ailment was," I explained looking out over the lake with my coffee cup in hand. I turned back to her with an unsure look on my face, "I still don't know if the UTI was the problem. But no matter, I'm just glad you're up and around. Hopefully we can get back to normal."

Cindy loaded the rest of her egg on the last half of her toast and took a bite, "Any thoughts on a job?"

"Yeah," I replied, suddenly realizing I hadn't said anything to Cindy about the prospects I'd been working on. It seemed whenever I got excited about a job in the past, I would somehow jinx it by talking about it too much. So this time I hadn't said anything about what I had applied for. I guess it was the hockey player superstition in me. "A couple of administrative positions have come up at the County that I've applied for," I began caving to the curse of the jinx again. "Both of them would be a good fit for my skill set. Lots of computer and organization work but dealing with people a lot as well. The new Aldi coming to town is also looking to hire a general manager. That position offers training for the candidate that would take place off location to begin with."

Cindy took hold of my hand gently and looked me right in the eye. "Honey, I know you can do any of those jobs and do them well. I have confidence in you," she said, squeezing my hand firmly. "God's going to take care of us."

I nodded in agreement, sort of. "You know, we're in that place again where only God can take care of us. No job, not much money, just the two of us and a blessed life full of the impossible that God has figured out time and time again. Our 33 years together have been all about God taking care of us, and I wouldn't trade it for anything."

"And he will do it again, honey. He will do it again," Cindy concluded in full confidence.

It's hard to describe the impact on a man when his wife is right there with him in the tough times. And God has given me the best helpmate on earth. She has been perfect for me and has completed me by pointing me again to who is really in charge, God himself.

I felt the puff of a gentle breeze make its way in the patio door by the breakfast table that morning. And with its exit, it took my hockey superstitions and carried them away, allowing me to share my burden with the helper God had provided for me: my dear wife.

The chicken coop was coming along nicely. Of course, if Cindy was in charge of the construction project, it would also be able to serve as a cottage that friends and family could stay in while visiting. But I was fine to settle for happy and content chickens.

Our day was a perfect combination of quality time spent together and working away on a project together. I was ready to start painting the chicken coop now that all the cracks and seams were caulked accordingly. If I had still been working, I'm sure the little structure wouldn't have received so much attention, and the same would have been true of Cindy. My heart was content to have followed the advice of our kids and enjoy the time together as Cindy gained her strength back from whatever ailment she had.

Wednesday began with rollers and the rest of an old can of white paint. I had cut in all the corners and hard-to-get-to spots on the chicken coop, so now it was time to make it shine with a full coat of paint. I was about to pour some of the time-thickened paint into my tray when my phone pinged indicating an email had come in. I reached into my back pocket, thinking it was perfect timing as I didn't have any paint on my hands yet.

The email read,

August 5, 2020
David Wall

Dear David:

Thank you for your interest in a position with Beltrami County.

We are scheduling interviews via our online self-scheduler. To self-schedule your interview, go to governmentjobs.com and sign in. Click on your name in the upper right, then Applications & Status. To the right of the job title click on Schedule Appointment and select a time slot for your interview.

I dropped my roller and read the email two more times just to make sure I read it right. I've got an interview with the County for the first job I applied for! I ran over to the house, burst through the door and announced the great news to Cindy, "Honey! I've got an interview with the County!"

"That's great news!" Cindy replied breathing a sigh of relief the chicken coop wasn't on fire or some other tragedy hadn't taken place. "When did you apply with the County?" She queried.

"This is the first position I applied for," I said excitedly, popping the lid open on the laptop. "I have to go online and schedule an interview as it says here in the email."

"Dave," Cindy said in that tone used when a wife has to ask a question of her husband a second time. "When did you apply with the County?"

"Oh yeah," I said, realizing Cindy was talking to me as I went to the website the email indicated. "Ummm…"

"Yes, the answer," my patient wife tried the third time.

"Ahh, this is the first position I applied for back on…" I diverted to check emails first to see the actual date of application because it had been a while ago. "Here it is," I stated quickly. "July 2nd I applied initially."

"You didn't say anything about applying back then," Cindy stated in a half questioning inflection.

"Yeah, I didn't want to jinx anything. I just kept the opportunity and application to myself," I confessed. "The position looks like a perfect fit for me. Lots of administrative work."

"That would be a good fit," Cindy agreed. "But don't ever be afraid to tell me what's on your heart, dear. I'll support you and cheer you on no matter what," she said in a way that enveloped me like the most comfortable blanket you could wrap yourself in on a cold winter's night, even though it was the beginning of August.

"Yeah, I have to self-schedule an interview," I said looking at the screen for the appropriate login links. "I'm gonna try to get in tomorrow or Friday at the earliest. We need to get the revenue stream flowing again as soon as possible," I said fully dialed into the task at hand. The chicken coop was a distant memory now, even if the paint can sat open in the morning sun.

"Well, I'm sure you'll do a great job no matter what," Cindy supported from over my shoulder as I finally reached the interview times available.

"Looks like the soonest time available is next week on Wednesday," I declared after double checking all the options. "Rats, I have to wait a whole week."

"Maybe the Lord just wants us to spend more time together," my ever-intuitive wife contributed. "I guess we just needed a full two weeks before you head back to work."

"I suppose," I agreed with a tinge of disappointment in my voice. "Not much we can do about it. I'm thankful, nonetheless."

Cindy cracked a cornered smile, "Better break out the suit and get it ready. Looks like you're interviewing for an office job."

"True that," I agreed and locked in the interview for the following Wednesday.

Back at the coop, I started rolling the first coat of paint while my mind was already in interview mode. I thought back 10 years when we returned home from nearly 20 years on the mission field. I hadn't really interviewed for a job before, so I was thankful for friends and family who gave me tips on how to dress and present myself. Now I was back in the same situation. My prayer was this would be the last interview of my working career.

At noon Cindy and I had a leisurely lunch, no rush to get back to the painting. But when I finally did get back at it something was amiss. Fatty, the largest of the hens, was by herself and perched on one of the sawhorses by the chicken coop. That was odd I thought to myself, she was like the ringleader and typically the others followed her around. I wondered where the others were, so I set out to find them. I looked everywhere and finally found them all tucked in under the raspberry bushes in another part of the yard, but two were missing. Suspecting some sort of ill will, I herded them back over to the coop and locked them inside. I headed to another part of the yard by our two small ponds in search of the remaining pair. Out of the corner of my eye, I spotted something white in the center of a trail off that side of the yard. I headed in that direction thinking it was a plastic bag or something, but soon realized it was a pile of feathers.

Unreal, I thought to myself. *Something grabbed one of the birds in broad daylight and had a quick take-out lunch!* Sure enough, it was the feathers of our only white hen neatly laid out in a circle. Whatever brought about her demise wasn't a messy eater! The feathers weren't scattered about in a violent fashion at all like the culprit was in a hurry. I would've sworn the job was done with meticulous precision with actual hands by how the feathers were laid out in the center of the trail. I continued the search for the second bird but couldn't find another pile of feathers anywhere on the surrounding trails.

Cindy was taking her afternoon nap, so I didn't break the news to her right away. I was just dumbfounded as to what would be hunting at high noon around the property. If you see a raccoon mid-day you are pretty much guaranteed it's rabid and should shoot it on the spot. Foxes don't typically roam during the day, more like early morning or early evening is their habitual hunting time. Just out of curiosity I headed over to my brother-in-law's to see if their dog had done the deed, but there was neither evidence of fresh blood on her nor were there any feathers around the garage. Typically, when she'd kill something, she would bring her trophy home and drop it right on the pavers in front of the garage doors. More like a cat thing, than a dog thing. But after a thorough inspection, I determined the crime wasn't committed by my dog-in-law.

Cindy got up from her nap, and I broke the news to her, detailing my investigation and the perplexing findings.

"Well, I guess you never know when calamity is going to strike," was her comment. "Who would've thought we'd lose a chicken in broad daylight?"

"Right," I agreed. "I guess I'll keep them locked up for a couple of days. Just in case the thief decides to come back again."

Towards evening after supper, we decided to let the chickens out again, but we sat out in the yard and watched them the whole time. The evening was pleasant for early August, and it was nice just to relax under the oak tree in the front yard. I had to chuckle to myself; I felt as if we were a couple of old fogies sitting out there watching the chickens chase bugs and peck away at the ground.

The time to be home the past couple of weeks was wonderful and much needed. Cindy was feeling much better and I had a job interview lined up, so I was confident God was going to take care of our needs once again. But there was just one thing out of place: Cindy was unusually quiet. Conversation is rarely difficult for the two of us. We always have something to discuss or talk about. But as the gentle evening wore on, I was a little unsettled about her disposition and how quiet she was. Her sullenness wasn't from losing the chickens earlier in the day as she wasn't that tied to them. No, it was different. It was as if something was suppressing her...I could see it in her eyes.

> *It was like something was suppressing her, I could see it in her eyes.*

As the sun lowered itself below the tree line, our friendly neighborhood mosquitos broke up the evening and escorted us back into the house. I put the chickens away and then joined Cindy inside for a card game to finish out the evening.

| day 0 continued
SAH

"My wife is having a seizure!" My lips quivered as I responded into my cell phone, which was lying on the floor. Cindy was frothing at the mouth and twitching all over. I held her on her side to prevent her from choking or swallowing her tongue.

"Tell me where your wife is right now and describe for me what is happening with her," the young dispatch on the other end asked with confidence in his voice.

"She's lying on the floor here in our bedroom. She got up to use the bathroom and then collapsed. I immediately saw she was convulsing and struggling to breathe. I've positioned her on her side so she wouldn't choke or swallow her tongue, and she's still in seizure," I chronicled as best I could in response.

"You're doing an excellent job so far," the dispatch encouraged. "Which side is she positioned on?" he queried.

"The right side," I came back.

"Ok, I'm going to have you roll her back over onto her left side for me," he instructed in a calm and yet hurried voice that knew time was of the essence.

It seemed to take forever to roll Cindy over, but I managed to get her repositioned on her left side. She was struggling for breath, gurgling with every gasp, and she was stiff with every muscle in her body involuntarily contracting. "Ok, I have her on her left side now," I managed to say in the direction of the phone.

Further encouragement came from the dispatcher's firm yet gentle voice, "You're doing excellent. Now when did the seizure start and does your wife have a history of seizures?"

As best I could I tried to measure the time and responded as I kneeled beside my still struggling wife, "I think we're about 4-5 minutes into the seizure and no history of them whatsoever."

"Ok, I'm dispatching the ambulance now and they'll be on their way. Looks like we have about 15 minutes for an ETA."

"I need to call my brother-in-law; he lives just down the laneway," I instructed the dispatcher.

"I'll do that for you!" The young man countered. "I want to keep you on the line. What's his number?"

I thought I had the number memorized, but with modern cell technology, you hardly know your own number anymore. With one arm holding Cindy I reached for my phone, pulling up my main contacts and reading the number to dispatch.

"Ok, I'm calling him now." And the line went silent for a few moments that seemed like a lifetime, but then the phone came to life again. "Your brother-in-law is on his way over. Update me on how your wife is doing."

"She's still in seizure and struggling for breath," I said.

You lose all track of time in situations like these, but suddenly my sister-in-law burst through the front door with Cindy's younger brother and nephew in tow. I can't express the feeling of relief that came over me when they arrived. Those initial moments were lonely and hopeless even though dispatch said I was doing great.

My sister-in-law Calandra is the administrator at the county jail, and over the years as she's worked her way up to that position, she has seen more than her fair share of emergencies with overdoses and inmates going into seizures from one thing or another. I immediately let her take over while giving a brief update of what happened.

"Dispatch, this is Cindy's sister-in-law," and she proceeded to give her name and badge number to ID herself. Immediately the dispatcher recognized her and the two made a connection as they continued a discussion in more detail about Cindy's condition.

I turned to give instructions to my nephew and started directing traffic. "The ambulance is on the way, so can you open the garage and back out the CRV? That way they'll be able to back right up and get close. Park the car over to the side out of the way."

I returned to the bedroom so thankful for the support as survivor's fog began enveloping me. While his wife was still in discussion with dispatch, Cindy's brother was on one knee beside her, praying for his sister, 12 years his senior. He always looked up to her. What a team, I thought, one taking care of the emergency and one interceding in support. I didn't realize it at the time, but while I was out directing traffic, Cindy had quit breathing, but Calandra managed to get her stimulated and breathing again.

Sirens could now be heard from the highway. Cindy began coming out of the seizure, coughing and squirming, followed by some other unpleasant bodily reactions to the trauma she was going through. We figured the seizure had lasted the better side of 10 minutes, so coming out of it was a struggle, to put it mildly.

The ambulance crew arrived, entering the house through the open garage. Calandra gave a fresh update as the pair of medics began assessing Cindy and hooking up their gear to measure her vitals. Cindy was semi-conscious now and resisted anything touching her with a wiping away motion, a natural reaction when coming out of a grand mal. I stood back and let things happen—as though time came to a standstill.

Before I knew it, Cindy was on the gurney and being wheeled through the garage to the back of the ambulance. Just before she entered it, I could see she was struggling to pull the sheet covering her further up her chest. I have a foggy memory of thinking Cindy was still alive, but she had no idea what was happening. She was just responding naturally to cover herself because of feeling cold.

The ambulance doors closed as one EMT joined Cindy in the back and the other took the steering wheel in the front. The unit began to roll in the direction of the ER in town, but it was all in slow motion.

My thoughts were in slow motion as well, slowing down and almost coming to a standstill. My wife just left without our customary kiss, hug and "I-love-you" goodbye. Something we did without fail. But today was a different day as I watched the flashing lights round the corner of the laneway.

"Dave!" Suddenly the fog dissipated, and I realized Calandra was holding my arm. "Get in your car and follow the ambulance. We'll take care of everything here," she instructed.

I blinked and looked down. I was still in my boxers. Later on, the thought came to me, *I certainly hope the barn door wasn't open the whole time!* But who cares, you don't think of things like that when in trauma.

"I better get some clothes on first," I mustered out of a small measure of mental cohesion. I found a pair of pants, a shirt and maybe even some socks.

And then of course the most important piece of "clothing" we all have now, my phone. I jumped in the car and headed to town.

Distracted driving took on a whole new meaning as I headed down the laneway to Little Turtle Road that connected me to County Rd 15 which led into town. I don't even remember the drive. I wasn't in the car. I was with my wife and her alone. I had no thoughts. I was just with her.

Pulling into the ER parking lot was familiar as I had just been here two weeks before…with my wife. Now she was here before me, and I was walking in alone.

One of the EMTs met me outside with an update, "Sir, your wife went into seizure again before we arrived, and she didn't come out of it. The ER doctor intubated her as fast as possible and got her on life support." I'm sure the news wasn't easy for the EMT to pass on, but I thanked him and proceeded through the automatic doors of the ER. I was amazingly calm and quiet as I answered all the COVID-19 questions and proceeded to the reception desk.

"My wife just came in by ambulance," I informed the gal at the desk.

"What are your wife's name and date of birth?" she asked following protocol as gingerly as she could manage.

"Cynthia Wall, W-A-L-L," I mechanically spelled out as I always do for clarity. "Birthdate is," and I proceeded to give her the date of birth.

"Okay, perfect," she answered with growing empathy in her voice. "We'll get you back there as soon as the doctor says it's okay."

"Thank you," I responded from behind my mask and took a seat in the waiting area.

It wasn't more than a few moments and I was barely back into my state of fog when the receptionist informed me, "Mr. Wall, you may proceed back to room number one."

I pushed my way through the large doors that separated the ER from the waiting room and stood outside room one. Inside I could hear a beehive of activity. I assumed I could just enter, so I cracked the door open and moved in. For a brief second all became silent as my eyes went directly to Cindy lying on the table, bare-chested with tubes and wires, and who knows what else hooked up to her.

"Are you the husband," a large, sort of overweight man asked from behind all his PPE.

"Yes, I am," I managed, still locked in on the lifeless form of my wife on the table.

"I'm Dr. So and So." I lost track of his name after the third syllable. "Let's step into the hall for a moment." I complied, turned back to the door and accompanied Dr. So and So.

"Your wife has experienced a subarachnoid hemorrhage (SAH) or aneurysm. When she arrived at the ER she was in her second full seizure and struggled to breathe; therefore we intubated her immediately."

My initial reaction was mild panic as intubation had developed a bad report over the past months because of all the COVID-19-related fatalities. But I let the doctor continue.

"Your wife is extremely critical, and I've ordered a medivac to our Fargo facility via helicopter. Time is of the essence as the CT shows a lot of blood in the brain cavity already. Fargo has an excellent neurology team and the expertise to provide the critical care she needs."

I nodded my head, "Let's do it." All the while praying to God, or should I say telling God, "You've really put us in the impossible this time, haven't you."

"If you'd like to come back in the room, I can walk you through the CT scan?" The kind doctor offered.

"Sure," I responded. "I'd appreciate that."

We entered the room again greeted by all the noises of life support. The doctor pulled up Cindy's CT scan and showed me the areas of the skull where blood had already filled in. As he explained the scan to me, I felt he was holding back from painting a picture of utter destruction. That was okay; he was making the right call to have Cindy airlifted. But I did find out subsequently the diagnosis was grave, and there was little chance for survival.

The door cracked open again, and it was Cindy's father. He knew exactly what was happening, and his countenance communicated it clearly. His first wife Betty, Cindy's mom, died 28 years ago this very week of the exact same thing, at the exact same age. He didn't want to have to go through this again in his lifetime.

> *Both in tears, we talked as men as I updated him on exactly what happened just a short time ago. "Chas," I began, "You know your mom's desire, don't you?"*

I left the room and my wife to the professionals and returned to the parking lot.

I'm not even sure at what point I had started calling the kids to let them know the situation, but I do remember talking to each one of them except Seth as he was under quarantine in downtown Sydney, Australia. I tasked Essie with trying to reach him. Maea lived in Fargo and was already headed to the hospital to meet the helicopter.

Chas was the closest to town and was already headed to the hospital from his work as a manufacturing engineer in a neighboring town. When he pulled into the parking lot, I met him, and we had the deepest hug. Both in tears, we talked as men as I updated him on exactly what happened just a short time ago. "Chas," I began, "You know your mom's desire, don't you?"

"Only too clearly," was his response. "She wouldn't want us to hold her back," he continued as the distant sound of the medivac chopper reached us from the south. "As hard as it is, I know Mom would much rather go be with Jesus than stay here, and I'm okay with that," he continued through his tears.

We both felt completely helpless to do anything but pray and prepare ourselves for the road ahead as the chopper swung down onto the helipad and landed. The engine was powered down, and the crew began jumping out in preparation for their patient, my dear wife.

By this time Cindy's dad had joined us again. "I don't want to stay and watch the chopper leave," I told the two of them. "I'm heading back home to pack a few items and then I'll meet you down in Fargo." I wasn't meaning to be cold about the whole situation transpiring; I just didn't want the vision of my wife being wheeled out, loaded in the chopper, and whisked off burned into my memory. If I was going to lose her, I wanted only the many years of great memories in my mind. I suppose my thoughts were the beginning of a coping mechanism, and that's okay. The day had only begun, and the sun wasn't going to set for a very long time.

Again, I'm not sure how my distracted driving got me back to our house, but when I turned down the laneway, I was greeted by another beehive of activity. First, as I saw the propane company's big boom truck backed up alongside the house, it dawned on me I had ordered a new propane tank double the size of the old one, and today was the day of installation.

Inside the house, Calandra and Cindy's sister, Chris were busy cleaning and getting some of Cindy's clothes set out for me to take to Fargo. "What's with the propane guy?" Chris asked me with a "that's-great-timing" tone.

"I ordered a new tank back mid-July because I don't want to burn wood anymore," I stated through the fog. "I guess I better throw a backpack together," I continued, trying to solve in my mind what seemed like a calculus equation—to figure out the number of boxers and socks I'd need to throw in my backpack. Little things suddenly became complicated in the rush to get on the road for the two-and-one-half-hour drive to catch up to the chopper's destination.

The floor of the bedroom needed attention from where Cindy lay fighting for her life. I stopped in my tracks and froze when I saw it. A gentle hand came to my shoulder. "Dave, don't worry about it," Calandra said graciously. "I'll take care of it. You just get on the road as soon as you can. You need to get to Fargo."

Chris worked away on pants, sweaters and socks for Cindy. I threw my clothes in a separate backpack. It was so good to have the help as my thoughts had become pretty myopic with the focus of getting to my wife. I did manage to turn the A/C off, leave instructions with Calandra about the chickens and button up a few other things in the house before heading out to the car.

I figured I better talk to the propane guy before taking off, so I went over to him as he was about to lift the new tank off the back of the truck. "Sorry about all the hustle and bustle, but my wife is being medevaced to Fargo as we speak," I explained thinking there was no time to candy coat anything.

"I'm so sorry," the poor guy responded in shock. "I had no idea. I can just do this another day if it helps."

"No, no," I assured him. "I want this bigger tank installed, so just do what you gotta do. Is there anything I need to sign before I hit the road?"

"Actually, there is a bit of paper you need to scratch your signature on," he began as he turned to grab his clipboard from the cab of the truck. "Oh, and will you leave the house open? I'll need to check the furnace once everything is hooked up and in place."

Locking the house? Hadn't thought of that. Who knew when I'd be back again. "Yeah, just go in through the side door in the garage and do what you need to do," I instructed as I signed the appropriate documents. I'm sure he explained all the paperwork to me, but my occupied mind was already down the road headed to Fargo.

The drive to Fargo was all too familiar as Cindy and I had driven it countless times to attend Maea's track events at North Dakota State. We pretty much had the journey timed down to the minute with the short cuts and places to stop for gas that were so much cheaper than Bemidji. We'd pass the two and one-half hours streaming podcasts and music. But today it was just me, and I was beginning what would turn out to be the fastest and longest road trip of my life.

Maea was waiting at the hospital with her husband Bryan and watched the helicopter fly in carrying her mother for what might be the last flight of her life on earth. The chopper swung in and landed on the 5th floor deck where the ICU ward doors swung open and countless personnel came out on the deck to receive the patient—our patient. I was so glad Maea was there, but I also felt for her as she was the only immediate family member until Chas, Jordan and I could get there.

The silence in the car was deafening as I headed back down the laneway and followed my GPS's blue line of direction. I popped in my Bluetooth earbuds and pulled up my favorite morning live stream, Glenn Beck. Normally, I drank in all of the conversations and analysis of what's going around the country, but this morning I didn't hear a thing. Sorry, Glenn.

As I drove, my heart and mind were mesmerized by each broken center line I passed by. When I learned as a teenager to drive on the highway, I remember my dad saying, "Dave, don't look directly at the lines on the road; they'll hypnotize you. Watch them only with your peripheral vision, and keep looking forward down the road." Today I couldn't help myself staring as each blip of yellow seemed to be a thought that came with a question I couldn't answer or explain. What if this had happened at three in the morning? I would've thought nothing more than Cindy bumped the door as we all do in the middle of the night navigating our way through the dark to the bathroom. I would've dozed off back to sleep only to wake in the morning to… the thought was chilling.

The center line suddenly turned solid yellow—the phone was ringing. I snapped out of my thoughts and glanced at the number on the phone sitting in the holder on the dash. I didn't recognize it and immediately thought it was a robocall about car warranty. *Better answer it anyway*, I thought to myself. I pushed the right-side earbud, "Hello."

It was an accented voice from the direction of India, "With whom am I speaking?"

"This is Dave," I politely responded wondering why the person hadn't immediately started in on the expiring car warranty spiel.

"David Wall?" the person questioned further.

"Yes, that is correct," I confirmed slowly, curious how they knew my last name.

"This is Dr. S from the Sanford Medical Center in Fargo," the voice began. Making sure I stayed on the right side of the solid line, I was now fully dialed in and listening. This was not a passing thought or memory or a car warranty gimmick. "Our neurosurgeon team here in Fargo has received your wife Cynthia into urgent care. Her situation is very grave. We'll need to perform several lifesaving measures, but I'll need your consent as we begin to implement a strategy for doing so."

"Yes, absolutely," I responded a little shocked they would even ask permission. But then again, I hadn't been through something like this before.

"First off," the Dr. continued, "Can you give me a brief timeline of what happened this morning?"

"Sure," I began without any consideration of lines on the road. I explained times and assessments and actions I had taken only a short time before not even realizing what the current time was.

"Ok, here is the first procedure we are going to do," the doctor continued. It had something to do with entering Cindy's femoral artery in the groin, doing an angiogram then injecting a dye into the brain cavity to perform a more accurate CT scan. I think. Pretty much everything the doctor said, including the risks, went completely over my head. "As Cindy's spouse, do we have your verbal consent to proceed knowing the risks I have just explained to you?"

He wanted my consent. "Yes, of course," I affirmed.

"Alright, we'll proceed and keep you updated," the Doctor concluded.

"Thank you, doctor," and I was back to the dotted lines somewhere down the road of a very different life.

But then the questions started up again. What if I hadn't gone back to bed this morning, but put the coffee on and done my normal routine of checking the chickens and enjoying the morning sun outside in the yard? And then it hit me. What if I'd gone to work and not returned until 7:00 p.m.?

"Dear God," I said out loud with tears now streaming down my face, blurring whatever lines there were I wasn't paying attention to anyway. I was now beginning to see God's hand come into place in this whole ordeal. My sons were faithful to sit me down and set my course straight allowing me to leave work only a couple of weeks prior giving Cindy and me some wonderful time together. It was as if the time was preparation for what would be the biggest trial of our lives. The tears began flowing even more as my heart overflowed in thankfulness to God. There is no way the ordering of events that had taken place was due to some random chaos of an impersonal power of the universe. No, God indeed is sovereign and had intervened in our lives in a way only his omniscience could do. I was being given the immense privilege of seeing firsthand the incredible blending of God's sovereignty and the responsibility of man working in tandem together. My sons made a choice to confront their father. I had a choice to respond to their correction. God took all the puzzle pieces and fit them together according to his design of the big picture. That is practical theology. That is relationship. That causes your heart to overflow in thankfulness.

I had to call Chas and tell him what had overcome me. He was also on the road by this time and he answered quickly, "Hey."

Through my tears, I said, "Thank you son for being faithful to God and sitting me down a couple of weeks back."

"Dad, are you sure you're able to drive?" He retorted immediately, concerned if I could even see the road through my sobbing.

"Yes, of course," I affirmed with a partial chuckle. "I'm just so thankful, I had to call you."

Chas didn't need any time to respond, "Yes, you can certainly see God's hand in this. His fingerprints are all over it, and that's a good thing."

"It's the best place to be," I agreed, sensing a peace in my heart amidst a turbulent sea of waves so far that morning. Suddenly the earpiece started beeping. Another phone call was coming in, and it looked similar to the earlier call from "India."

"Chas, it looks like the doctors are calling again. Better go."

"Hello, this is Dave," I answered, willing to give my name right away this time.

"David Wall? Are you the husband of Cynthia Wall?" the lightly accented voice asked, which I later found out was Pakistani.

"Yes, I'm Cindy's husband," I affirmed.

"This is Dr. D and I need to explain the next procedure for your wife's lifesaving treatment," the doctor disclosed as once again I was surprised, they needed my permission.

The doctor began his explanation in a similar fashion as the first doctor, "Cynthia's subarachnoid hemorrhage has filled the brain cavity with a critical amount of blood causing a potentially lethal intracranial pressure." The doctor went on to explain how he'd have to insert a drainage apparatus into Cindy's skull to relieve the pressure, and then he continued with the risks involved in the procedure. "May I have your verbal consent to proceed, sir?" The doctor concluded.

Everything just explained to me went completely over my head again, but that didn't matter at this point. The situation was urgent. "Yes, of course. Please proceed!"

"Thank you, we'll proceed accordingly," and the doctor ended the call.

I returned to the broken lines that kept coming and coming, and although they mean you can pass, I couldn't pass the thoughts flooding my mind. How perfect Jordan and his family had just moved back to the area a month prior.

He was only a quick trip away and was already on his way to meet us at the hospital.

I thought I should call Joni, Cindy's lifelong friend here in Bemidji. I had her on speed dial and she answered the phone knowing it was me calling. "Yes, Mr. Wall, what's up?"

"Joni," I began without being able to control the quiver in my voice. "Cindy had an aneurysm this morning and has been airlifted to Fargo."

"No, no, no!" she came back in a voice trembling more than mine. "Dave, what happened, and is she going to make it?"

"I'm not sure at this point, but doctors in Bemidji knew it was severe enough they summoned the helicopter soon after arrival at the ER. She was already in her second seizure at that point and they put her on life support immediately," I explained as Joni's tears were flowing through my phone cascading with mine and falling down my cheeks.

"Oh my, I can't bear the thought of losing her," Joni continued.

I knew only too well the depth of their friendship. "I thought I should call you first outside of family, Joni. You mean so much to her," I added as another call was coming in. It was the number the doctors in Fargo were using. "Looks like another update is coming from the doctors. Better take it."

"Hello, this is Dave," I answered, now welcoming the chance to hear another Indian accent on the other end.

"David, this is Dr. S with another update for you," he began. "How far out are you now?"

"I'd say just over an hour I guess," I responded, not caring about the distance as I wanted the update.

"Ok, Dr. D has successfully inserted the drainage device and we are relieving the intracranial pressure now. We have located the hemorrhage, and now we need to do a procedure called coiling. This procedure is intravascular where we actually go into the brain and seal the aneurysm with platinum thread to stop the hemorrhage," the doctor explained. I couldn't even imagine what he was talking about. Coiling? Sealing? Platinum thread? No cutting the skull open and going in? The doctor went through the risks and then concluded, "May I have your verbal consent to proceed?"

"Yeah, for sure. Please proceed," I said in a clueless state of wonderment. "And thank you so much for trying to help my wife."

"Thank you and we'll get started on prepping for the procedure." And with that the doctor hung up.

By this time the rest of the journey was four-lane highway, and before I knew it, I arrived in Fargo, pulling into the ER parking lot of the new castle-looking fortress of a hospital owned and operated by Sanford Health. The structure had ten floors made up of four wings giving it the shape of a large "X" from the air. I looked up to the fifth-floor helipad on the north side where they had brought Cindy upon arrival. My mind was numb as I imagined her being removed from the aircraft and taken inside. We see and hear medivacs all the time, but this time it was personal, too personal.

Maea came out of the ER entrance and met me at the doors. You can't even talk when you see your children in such situations. You just hug and cry.

"Chas and Jordan are on their way and should be here soon," I managed to say.

"We are just waiting to be taken up to the actual waiting area on the third floor," Maea gently instructed. She was strong, and she freely passed a measure along to me.

Chas arrived shortly after, and we waited together for a time on ground level, and then were taken up to the third floor waiting area where we could all sit together and wait. Fifth floor was the actual ICU level, but because of COVID-19 restrictions, we were permitted to wait as a group only in this area on third.

The kids were on and off their phones talking with Essie in Florida and Jordan who was just pulling into the parking area and getting instructions on how to meet up with us. Essie and Travis had already booked flights for themselves and the girls and would be leaving Tampa at about 4 p.m. They figured an ETA of 3 a.m. into Fargo.

None of the kids had yet been able to reach Seth. It was sometime in the middle of the night in Sydney, Australia where they were holed up in quarantine since arrival 11 days prior. I felt so bad for him, hoping his first phone call wasn't with the news his mother didn't make it. But no matter when he'd finally get the news, he and his family were stuck in quarantine awaiting release to head on to Tasmania where they would make their home. I figured if the worst happened, he'd get special permission to fly back for his mom's funeral.

The waiting area held several other families and loved ones of patients all facing their own set of circumstances. I sat wondering what their stories were and if they were similar to ours. What kind of grief and loss were they facing on this day of days?

Maea found out from the receptionist the procedure should be done inside of an hour, so we waited together and whittled the time away with light discussion and stories. There were display boards that showed doctors' names and the progress of their unnamed procedures. Each one was coded with language we didn't understand, and as the doctors' names moved toward the top of the screen, we figured progress was being made. The screens were similar to the ones you find at the airport displaying flight arrivals and departures, something our family found familiar with all the traveling we had done together around the world. There was just one problem we noticed, our doctor's name wasn't moving up the screen.

"Is anybody hungry?" Chas asked of the group in a quiet voice. I hadn't thought of eating considering the circumstances, but it was now about 2 p.m., and I hadn't had anything to eat yet.

"I'd be up for something quick," I affirmed. "What about Jimmy John's? They are Freaky Fast and Freaky Fresh," I added for a bit of humor to lighten the heaviness of the hospital waiting room. Without another word, the three guys had their phones out looking at the menus and locations of the sub shop.

"There's one not too far from here," Jordan offered. "What sounds appealing to you all? Chas and I can go get everyone's order."

"I'll take the #7 East Coast Italian," I said, revealing my obvious familiarity with the JJ menu. "But be sure to hold the onions," I instructed. "I don't want to be breathing those into my mask for the rest of the day."

So with my order and orders for Maea and Bryan, the two boys were off to fetch us some food. It did my heart good to see the two of them leave together. Both were in their thirties now and had been separated by life, careers and rearing families. My thoughts flashed back to them growing up in the jungle together where they were never separated. Each day was an adventure of fishing and hunting with the tribal kids. Both were fluent in three languages and were a tremendous part of our work as they provided a bridge of commonality with the people we worked among. But today they had been brought back together for a not-so-pleasant reason. And with that thought, I was back to the reality of awaiting the unknown.

The hour of waiting turned into three and a half hours. We all wondered if we heard something wrong about how long the procedure would take, but finally, Dr. S's name made it to the top of the digital board and read "post-op." I didn't want to be a doubter, but I knew in my heart something was wrong with having to wait so long. A nurse finally showed up at the waiting room and said we were free to go up to room 546 in ICU and see Cindy, but with instructions that only two were allowed in the room at a time.

| day 0 continued
ICU

I don't even remember who went to the room with me first; I just wanted to see my dear wife whom I hadn't seen since about 7 a.m. The journey up to fifth floor ICU seemed to take as long as the drive from home, as I had no idea what to expect upon arrival. I made my way down the meandering ward following the instructions of how to get to room 546. I cracked open the door, and as I slowly entered, I was greeted by a buzz of monitors flashing, fluid pumps pumping, nurses doing their urgent care business and then the rise and fall sound of the life support that had kept Cindy alive since reaching the ER. Tubes and wires seemed to go in every direction, all attached to Cindy in some fashion and performing a function I would soon learn about in detail.

I went to the side of the bed and just looked at my wife. She was lifeless and swollen from all the fluid being pumped into her. Her chest was involuntarily rising and falling as the ventilator pushed air and oxygen through the endotracheal tube inserted into her mouth down to her windpipe. I took her hand which was slightly warmer than death and stood quietly. I couldn't talk. My words were trapped inside, and I couldn't get them out, but the noise in my heart and mind was much louder than the noise of the ICU room.

A young and fit nurse broke through the noise and handed me a plastic medicine jar from the other side of the bed. I wasn't sure what it was until she explained, "I went ahead and took her rings off," she began. "I've seen it where they've had to be cut off because of all the swelling."

I received the jar with a mumbled thanks and wondered if I'd ever get to put the rings back on my wife again. I was about to turn my attention back to Cindy when two doctors showed up at the door.

The doctors clad in their light blue scrubs made their way toward the bed. "Mr. Wall?" the shorter doctor asked from behind his mask.

"Yes, I'm Dave," I replied leaving Cindy's side hoping for an update as to how everything went over the past several hours. I was prepared with some questions and ready to explain our view of extended life support knowing that would be a topic of discussion.

It's hard to match physical descriptions from a voice over the phone, and I couldn't have imagined what these two neurosurgeons looked like who called me on the drive down. Dr. S was short and stocky and carried the heavier Indian accent. Dr. D was tall with broad shoulders. Both were heavily bearded, and both shared a border of origin and animosity—Pakistan and India. Only in America could you bring a skilled team together of this caliber to pursue your dreams and work in unity.

"I am Dr. S, the neurovascular surgeon for your wife, and this is my co-neurosurgeon Dr. D," he began. "We'd like to walk you through how treatment went with your wife if that is okay."

I didn't hesitate, "Absolutely, please."

And so the good doctor began, "Mr. Wall, your wife came in at the highest critical assessment level possible for a subarachnoid hemorrhage— level 5. After talking on the phone and listening to you describe the events of the morning, there is no doubt in my mind your actions have saved your wife's life."

My knees went weak. I shrugged my shoulders and looked at the floor. *That's quite a statement,* I thought to myself. *I just did what any husband would do in that situation.*

I managed to say aloud, "Well, I appreciate your words doctor, but many hands have gotten us to this point." I didn't want to be rude, but for me, credit was due in many other directions.

The doctor continued, "Dr. D was responsible for the insertion of the External Ventricular Drain which got the mounting intracranial pressure (ICP) under control. The ventricles in your wife's brain cavity were completely full of blood, which is what is fatal in this type of situation. Dr. D had minimal time for placement of the EVD when your wife arrived via airlift this morning."

I looked Dr. D in the eyes and nodded affirmation and thanks.

"Once the ICP was under control we were able to do the angiogram to assess the location of the hemorrhage and proceed with the seal, or coiling, to prevent further bleeding," the doctor explained. He drew a rough diagram on the whiteboard the nurses used for notes located just inside the door of the room. "The seal took right away and looked successful, so we removed all the gear back out of the femoral artery. But then our imaging showed the vessel ruptured again in another spot and started hemorrhaging." Right then it struck me why the procedure took so long; Cindy had a second aneurysm in the OR. The doctor continued, "We had to go back in immediately and seal off that hemorrhage as well. Thankfully it happened right there instead of post-op."

I just stood there wide-eyed until my initial response was able to work its way out of my mouth, "So what is the prognosis?"

The doctor was direct and honest with me, "Mr. Wall, we don't have a prognosis. We've been able to do all we know how to do. The seals look good, but with her critical arrival status and the second hemorrhage, we'll just have to wait and see how she does."

I didn't hesitate with my second question, "So what about damage? If my wife can't enjoy her grandkids, she won't want to come back."

"We cannot access the damage at this point," the doctor began, so willing to answer my questions. "We will have to keep her heavily sedated initially so the brain has optimum opportunity to heal. Once we feel it is safe to begin checking her response ability, we will."

> The doctor was direct and honest with me, "Mr. Wall, we don't have a prognosis. We've been able to do all we know how to."

I appreciated the doctor's willingness to explain the situation to me without painting a rosy picture of Cindy's grave situation, but I had a third and final question, "Doctor, what if she takes a turn for the worse? With two hemorrhages and the amount of pressure she's already faced, would a quality of life recovery even be possible at that point?"

"That is a good question, Mr. Wall," he began, not showing the slightest annoyance. He understood I was trying to get a footing in my heart and mind to cope with the situation at hand. "If she goes downhill any further, the likelihood of a recovery without issues is very minimal."

I didn't want to sound calloused or uncaring in what I was about to say to the doctors, but Cindy and I had both settled long before this time our desire not to be kept on life support unnecessarily. We firmly believe our accounts are settled with God through what is explained in the Bible. Jesus died, was buried and rose again guaranteeing God the Father was satisfied with his work of bearing the sins of the world and making full payment for all who would believe. We weren't afraid to die. Actually, over the past year, Cindy said to me several times, "I'm getting to the age my mom was when she passed away; better treat me well this next year." I shrugged her prediction off thinking she was built much more like her father than mother, unfortunately now I knew differently. Nonetheless for us to live had meaning and purpose, a win. If we were to die, we gain by going to live with God for eternity, a win. Life was a win-win all around because of our faith in God's Word.

"Doctor," I began after what seemed like forever gathering my thoughts, "My wife and I have a firm belief about life and death. We are secure in that belief. We knew we might face the possibility of this situation as Cindy's mother died of the same issue."

The doctor politely interrupted, "There is a family history of aneurysms?"

"Yes," I responded, realizing I had missed pointing that out somewhere in the course of the discussion. "Cindy's mother passed away 28 years ago this week at the same age."

"Why wasn't your wife ever screened?" the doctor said, showing the first sign of any exasperation.

"We didn't know you could be screened. There weren't any symptoms we could put a finger on or that indicated something was wrong. The only issue before today was a UTI that made her sick the last couple of weeks, at least that is what the diagnosis indicated," I stated in mild defense.

I could tell the doctor was perplexed about us not exercising the opportunity for preventative screening, but it was too late to worry about that now.

"Doctor, if Cindy takes a turn for the worse, her desire would be to let her go and not bring her back. I support her in that desire." Coming back half alive was not an option for us. The old adage, "Is the cup half full or half empty?" was not relevant in this situation. If you come back half-dead, you're just that—half dead. Cindy loved to live life, and if she couldn't live it fully alive, she'd rather gain by going on to eternity to be with her Savior. I continued with my thoughts aloud for the doctor, "Doctor on a scale of 1-10, with 10 meaning you keep the heartbeat going at any cost, we are about a two." Again, I was afraid of coming across as uncaring for my wife, but I was advocating for Cindy, and putting it on a scale for the doctors was the best way to communicate that in my mind.

The doctor was empathetic to our position and seemed quite impressed with my ability to be so decisive in such a situation. "I understand," he began nodding his head in agreement. "We'll order the DNR (Do Not Resuscitate) for her status." He turned to the nurse to confirm our desire, and a purple bracelet was attached to Cindy's wrist unbeknown to her, but an action she would have been in complete agreement with.

The doctor continued, "In our professional opinion, we would recommend keeping your wife on life support for 48 hours. It will give her a fighting chance. At that point, we will extubate her and be able to assess her survivability. If she survives, she will have at least three weeks of recovery in ICU."

I nodded in agreement and thanked the doctors as they left the room for their excellent care. I turned back to Cindy and made my way over to the bedside realizing I'd made the most significant decision of my life. And I also realized, while the decision didn't carry the sting of death, it still carried the sorrow and grief of possibly losing my best friend in life.

Over the next several hours the kids rotated in and out of the room to spend time with their mom. Each one was in tears, but each one carried the strength of hope their mom was okay with leaving us if that was the plan. As hard as it was, it was a beautiful display of grieving and peace with the possibility of losing a parent who had invested so much in them over the years.

Towards evening the kids all went over to Maea and Bryan's place, leaving me the last hour of ICU visiting time to be alone with Cindy. I stood by her bed holding her hand, now immune to all the sounds of life support. This was my time with my wife of 33 years. This was my time to talk with her, and so I began, "Honey, we have talked for years about a day like this. We prepared for this together. I guess you just got here first. And what I'm about to say to you, you would also say to me if I were on life support." I paused, wondering if I could say it to her. I didn't want to be a callous and cold husband, but what I said next was what we had agreed to say if either of us found ourselves in the position where survival was possible only with the help of a machine. "You are free to go. I won't hold you back. We have had a wonderful life together and done so much as a team and a couple. The kids all understand and support us in this. You are free to go spend eternity with your Savior. It is your gain." I didn't think I had any more tears to cry, but they didn't hold back in reserve as they flowed down my face following the freshly worn cascade from the previous hours of the day.

The time alone with Cindy was also my time to talk with God, or more accurately negotiate with God. The proper term would be to advocate or intercede. I began talking with our Maker as I had seen people in the Bible do when they went before God on another's behalf. Both Cindy and I treated our relationship with God personally—so personally, we believe the Bible when it says we can come before Him in boldness or confidence because of what His Son has done on our behalf. Therefore, I was clear in my negotiation on behalf of my wife as I began laying out the parameters or terms of what I was about to discuss. "Dear Lord, you know that in no way do I want to prevent You from accomplishing Your will and purpose through the events of this day. I am at peace with whatever You decide. If you want to take my wife to be with You, I know You will help me get through it and sustain me afterward. I also know it would be her gain to be with You. I know I don't have to give You permission, but I'm ok with that plan if that's what You desire. But dear God if You desire to have Cindy stay, I beg of You on her behalf, bring her back one hundred percent. She would not want to return halfway. She would desire to come back and live for You a hundred percent. I'm standing before You on behalf of Cindy, advocating for her."

I can't put in words the peace that came over my soul at that point. I somehow had confidence I had presented the desire of Cindy's heart before God, her Maker and He heard and understood my heart. The opportunity was precious and real. The opportunity allowed me to bare my soul to my Creator and Lord and ask Him to either take her one hundred percent or bring her back one hundred percent, a win-win.

As I stood alongside my wife while the clock in the room continued its march toward the end of visiting hours in the ICU, there was one more thing I felt compelled to do: sing my death song.

When we lived in the tribe in Papua New Guinea, we learned all too well what a death song was. In our study and acquisition of both the language and culture of the people, we had front row seats to the good, the bad, and the ugly of every aspect of the lives of those people. The good was how they lived their lives and survived in the rainforest. The bad was no different from our culture and all its vices. The ugly was the same too, and how they dealt with death is something I will never forget.

You always knew when someone had died in the village because of the eerie wailing that would begin. Typically, the wailing would begin before sunrise and travel through the jungle like a pervasive mist until it reached every ear. Sometimes the death was expected, and sometimes it wasn't. It didn't matter, because the hopeless wailing was always the same as it indicated death was no respecter of persons, and when it was ready to perform its nasty work, there was nothing that could be done to stop it.

All people in the village would show some type of remorse for the individual who passed, but the closest family showed an intense way of grieving like nothing we had ever seen in our culture. It may have been a wife, husband, son, daughter, brother, sister, or parent, but when a close relative showed up to where the body lay, the display of grief was powerful. They would begin singing their death song for the deceased mixed with flowing tears, wailing and rolling on the ground in sorrow. Their song would commence with the beginning of their relationship with the dead person and then carry through describing their lives together. The living relative would continue singing, ascending the ladder of the house, and then at first sight of the deceased would throw himself on the body in a crescendo of exasperation and unimaginable grief. The display was powerful and gripping. These people knew how to mourn, unlike our culture, limited to quiet hugs and tears caught by a soft tissue before embarrassing others gathered to share in the loss of a loved one. All shame and concern about onlookers are put aside in mourning expressed in the tribe, as hopelessness gripped those left behind.

Over time as we progressed in our understanding of the language and culture of the people, we were able to communicate with them the hope of the gospel found in God's Word, the Bible. Many came to place their trust in God's provision of salvation through the work of Jesus on the cross and gained confidence that one day they would be reunited with loved ones. The death songs were still sung, but many now ended their songs with the hope of seeing their loved ones again.

I had sung only one death song in my life, and it was when my father passed away in 2006. From what I had learned in the tribe, I had to express my grief over my father in the same way I had seen in the tribe. Now, I didn't roll on the ground or drape myself over his body, but I did stand alongside him, with tears rolling down my cheeks and sorrow in my heart, and sang through his life in the tribal language. My song included the journey of our lives together and how at that time he was an alcoholic, but God had intervened in his life and changed him completely. When my song was finished, I felt satisfied. I was able to mourn sufficiently for the greatest supporter of my life on this earth—my dad.

I involuntarily began my death song for Cindy, chronicling our lives together, but after a few stanzas I was suddenly stopped as if God was waving his hand in front of my face saying, "Wait, Dave. Just wait." So, I stopped. It wasn't time to sing my life story with Cindy yet.

The minute hand had worked its way to the top of the clock, and it was time to leave; visiting hours were over and the end of a very long day had come.

| day 1
waiting

That first night was stingy with its allowance for sleep. My mind was like a tennis ball in the world's longest volley being played on the hardest court surface available. I was hurled back and forth by the racket of facing life as a widower only to be returned by the racket of survival and the impending complications that could come with it. With each skillful return, a new spin was applied in an effort to outwit the opponent on the other side of the duel. Consciously or not, my body twisted with each move of the ball, allowing no time for quality rest. I didn't want to doubt God when faced with either extreme of the possibilities before me. If Cindy didn't make it, I was at peace with the option, but I felt the urge to begin planning—everything. If Cindy did make it but had complications, I worried she wouldn't forgive me if she were incapacitated. In her mind, it would be an honor to leave this earth as her mother had nearly three decades before. The match in my mind went into extra sets without a clear winner in the end. I longed for morning to come even though my energy had been spent on the court of my turbulent mind. I just wanted it to be morning and face what it would bring.

My restless grasp at sleep did have a welcome interruption at about 3 a.m. Chas and I were sharing opposite ends of Maea's large living room couch when the door creaked open, and in came the Floridians, Essie and

Travis. Two little girls were nestled into their shoulders searching for sleep after a long day of hopping between airports and the final stretch of road travel from the Twin Cities. Their interruption to my volleyed mind was welcome, and I enjoyed deep hugs from the exhausted travelers. It was now time for them to try to find their own measure of rest before facing the morning poking its head up just beyond the horizon.

Essie's arrival matched the rising sun that finally greeted us in the morning. Her energy and love of life can't help filling any dismal room. It's not that the other three kids weren't an encouragement to me the day before; it's just that Essie brings another whole set of gifts to the table wrapped in creativity with her personality.

From Maea's place we were only five minutes from the hospital...or seven minutes if we stopped at the Holiday gas station for an unbearable cup of their morning coffee. So, Essie and I made the quick journey with a stop on the way. Essie passed on the coffee and grabbed a muffin. She beat me to the counter not allowing me to pay, much to the delight of the older lady working the counter.

"Wow, you don't see kids treating their parents too often nowadays," the lady offered with eyebrows raised in amazement.

"Yeah, I guess I did something right to earn that, eh?" I replied, realizing I must be pretty tired as that's when my Canadian accent slips out. It was the first of several days the cashier would start the morning with us.

Each one of our kids is unique and has gifts and abilities they carry with them. Essie has an uncanny ability to brighten your day when you meet her. When she entered Cindy's room, she was in tears as her siblings were when they first saw their mother and the condition she was in. But with Essie, the morning sun broke through the hospital window as it does through thick clouds after a hard rain. The room brightened and came alive as Essie took to Cindy's bedside and began talking with her mom as if nothing were wrong, as if they were starting a craft project together.

"Hey Mom, it's Essie!" she began in a crisp morning tone. "Trav, the girls and I got in pretty late last night, but not to worry, we are just super glad our trip connected so well to get here to be with you," she continued as she held her mom's hand and gently caressed her arm.

Essie carried on her one-sided conversation while I took the opportunity to get an update from the ICU nurse. "How did the evening go?" I asked Molly, the current nurse on duty.

"I just came on an hour ago," the fit young nurse began as she went about her duties. Cindy was one of her two patients for the shift she was doing. Because it was the ICU, two patients keep a nurse pretty busy. "From the briefing of the night shift it looks like everything was pretty stable, but of course she is sedated so she can't wake up or move at all."

"So, you mean she could wake up if she wanted?" thinking she was in a coma as a result of the aneurysm.

"No, she's in what you would call 'on the street' a medically-induced coma," Molly explained, turning to the pump labeled 'propofol.' "The propofol keeps her sedated and therefore she can't wake up while under maintenance of that. It's for her protection during this critical 48-hour period."

"I see," I confirmed slowly as my mind suddenly triggered memories of Michael Jackson. "Can you explain to me the read-outs of the monitor?" I asked out of curiosity.

The obvious multitasker of a nurse was patient enough to explain each of the lines to me, knowing it would help me cope through the coming days. I must admit a lot of the explanation went over my head, but I sure appreciated the lesson nonetheless.

"Ok, the top line is heart rate, and as you can see it's a little high, but so are the rest of her readings with the body under duress," she began, with the sound of enjoyment to explain things to a curious mind. "The second line is the blood pressure; currently we want to see the systolic number under 200."

"Two hundred?" I gasped noticing it was currently in the mid-170 range. "Yikes!" I said under my breath. I would have thought it should be way lower, but apparently not in a critical state.

The nurse continued, "This line is oxygen saturation, and under that is respirations, which of course the ventilator is controlling for her."

"Yeah, the ventilator deal scared me yesterday morning with all the COVID stuff going on," I interjected.

"I understand," the nurse said with empathy in her voice, but continued on. "This second to last line is the critical one we are the most interested in—the ICP or intracranial pressure." A seriousness came over the nurse's countenance. "It's sitting at 18 currently, and we don't want to see it go over 20. The lethal issue with an aneurysm, as I'm sure you are well aware, is the build up of pressure in the head."

"Exactly," I agreed, realizing the lesson was a great reprieve and put me in the world of a medical student for a short time. "The drainage will mitigate that pressure accordingly?" I queried.

"Yes, the EVD, as we call it, is inserted into the ventricle on one side of the brain and drains via gravity into the tube on the other side of the bed," the nurse stated, pointing to the stand on the left side of Cindy's bed. "Come over here to this side, and I'll show you how this works and is monitored."

We rounded the foot of the bed still hearing a mix of ICU sounds and Essie's continued conversation with Cindy. "There's a reason the bed is marked with the sign 'Only RN's to Adjust Bed Height,' and that's because of this drain right here," my instructor pointed out. "We have the gravity flow set at 15 because we want to make sure the drain is the proper setting for pressure mitigation and draining blood, but not draining cerebral and spinal fluid. At this setting, we don't want to go over 20 ml of discharge an hour measured into this tube right here." She pointed to the discharge tube with her rubber-gloved hand. "When the tube measurement is full, we simply drain it into this holding bag by opening the valve below."

I followed the explanation down past the discharge tube and just stared frozen in my thoughts at what I saw. The bag was already more than half full of a mix of blood and what I assumed to be cerebral and spinal fluid. "Dear God," I said to myself inside my lips. Looking at Cindy from the outside you wouldn't know the battle that raged inside her head yesterday morning. But here hanging in a plastic collection bag was the aftermath of a bloody war that was fought over her life.

The nurse snapped me out of my thoughts concluding her lesson for the day, "Thus, the sedation these first 48 hours will keep Cindy from moving, especially sitting forward, as that would exacerbate the pressure in her skull, causing unnecessary discharge."

With all the explanations the nurse offered, my own ICP was pretty much over 30 now, but I was thankful for her willingness to explain so much, as I settled into the room for the next three weeks. I did have one further question for my competent teacher, "Did you do your nursing at North Dakota State here in Fargo?"

"I most certainly did!" the nurse shot back in Bison pride.

"That's awesome! Our daughter ran track for NDSU," I volunteered with my own measure of Bison pride.

"I ran track too!" the nurse said excitedly. "What's her name?"

"Maea, Maea Wall," I stated.

"Get out of town!" The RN came back with a sound of shock. "I know Maea! We ran together our first two years, but then I left the team to concentrate more on my nursing studies."

"Well, I'm glad you did!" I affirmed. "Because you are doing an awesome job here, and I'm glad you are with us during these critical hours."

"It's all my pleasure. And will I get to see Maea sometime today?" She asked in hopeful anticipation.

"She should be over here before long. I'll shoot her a text and let her know you are working," I said, pulling out my phone and turning back to the bedside, seeing as the lesson of the day had concluded. Later when Maea showed up, she and the nurse had a hug in a perfect blend of empathy and professionalism that was impressive and comforting for us as a family.

It's amazing how time flies when you're not having fun. Before Essie and I had much time with Cindy, our phones began buzzing with texts and calls from the other kids and close family hoping for a chance to see Cindy. None of us knew at this point whether she would make it or not, so we began organizing two-person bedside visits that would carry on throughout the day.

Essie began chatting with nurse Molly about getting the grandkids up to see their Grammy. Along with the two-person-at-a-time limit, there was a restriction against 18-and-under kids coming up to the ICU units. Thankfully, the nurse was able to work with her lead nurse on the ward and get permission for at least Essie's girls to come up. The concession was limited to a one-hour visit per child accompanied by a parent or set of two children if the younger was under two years of age. At least that's what we understood. The permission only pertained to Essie's girls, but we unknowingly applied it to all of Jordan's kids with hopes of also extending it to Chas's kids, who were scheduled to arrive after lunch from Bemidji.

Because of COVID-19 restrictions, our soon-to-be-growing group of family and friends had to remain outside the hospital, so we commandeered a couple of picnic tables at the west end of the facility. The location was perfect, tucked in under an overhang out of the elements of the weather. The location quickly became our little command center for changing out visitors, eating meals and entertaining all the grandkids. I'm sure people wondered if a daycare had set up shop, as each day there was a range of events going on like corn hole games, croquet out on the nearby grass and soccer matches between dads and kids. With such a large group there was a constant entourage of little boys being taken to the bathroom and diapers being changed for the younger kids. Meals were eaten together and ranged from home-cooked crockpot delights to Chick-fil-A ordered in by friends of Essie's from Florida.

Before the day's first visitors were changed out, two electroencephalogram or EEG technicians arrived in the room to set up Cindy's 24 hours of brain activity monitoring. The pair were super friendly and worked great as a team attaching 30 some electrodes to Cindy's scalp to cover as much brain activity as possible. Each electrode was fastened with some sort of glue assuring they were held in place, and by the time they were done, Cindy looked like Medusa or like she was getting the fanciest hair streaking job ever. Once the leads were all affixed, the technicians tested the monitor showing all electrical activity her brain would produce over the next day, which wasn't a lot. With the placement of the EEG, we now had to maneuver our way through another piece of equipment arranged around Cindy and her ICU bed. Even though it was cramped and tight, making me feel as if I were going to bump something and set off an alarm at each turn, I was appreciative of all that was being done to save the life of my wife.

The revolving door of little visitors began shortly after the technicians with each of the grandkids taking a turn to visit Grammy. Some were too young to understand what was happening, but all knew their Grammy didn't look right hooked up to all the different things in the room. Each one was quiet and somber, displaying great concern for their grandmother as she lay motionless without any response to their visits.

The time rotating the grandkids took all the way to 3:00 p.m., when a text came down from Jordan in Cindy's room, "No more under 18's allowed. Nurses wondered why so many children had been brought up."

Essie quickly shot a text back, "What about Addy? They are only a few minutes out."

"Nope, they are firm. No more kids." Jordan shot back with a sad face imoji.

Our hearts sank as a group. Cindy by no means played favorites with our grandkids; she loved them all with a full measure of attention. But Chas' little Addy had spent the most time with Grammy because she lived in Bemidji and because Cindy watched them all last year. The two had a special bond. Cindy had walked Addy through a thorough and complete understanding of God's plan of salvation, and Addy was clear about placing her trust in Jesus' work for her on the cross. I felt like crying knowing Cindy's sweet Addy may not get to see her Grammy again on this earth.

I was back up in Cindy's room about 4:00 p.m. when Dr. D entered with yet another doctor in tow. The two doctors started getting updates from the nurses and then made their way to the foot of the bed where Dr. D engaged us with the reason for his rounds, "We are 24 hours in and halfway to the goal of extubating Cynthia tomorrow afternoon. I'd like to go ahead and do a response test now to see how she is doing."

I'm sure the look on my face gave the doctor permission to do whatever, but I asked out of sheer ignorance, "How do you do that?"

"It's quite simple actually," the doctor began from behind his mask as I wondered how many he changed out on a daily basis. "We will back off the propofol which is keeping her sedated and when she wakes up enough, we'll run her through a few commands and see how she responds."

Confusion suddenly enveloped me, "What do you mean by wake her up?"

The doctor was patient and provided clarification on the propofol, "The propofol has a short half-life, so when we stop its administration, Cindy will begin to wake up in 5-10 minutes tops. When we see she is ready, we'll ask her some questions, and see how she responds."

It seemed so simple to me. "How long will you keep her awake?" I wondered aloud.

"Not long at all. As soon as we are done, we'll sedate her again," the doctor concluded, giving the nod to the nurse to back off the propofol.

I appreciated the willingness of the doctor to explain things so I could understand, but I had no clue as to what was going to happen. So, I just watched and let the medical team do their thing.

The nurse cut the flow of the sedative and sure enough, within a few minutes, Cindy's silent frame began to move. It was as if life began to flow back into her veins as she began to make slight movements from side to side. You could almost hear the creaking of her joints as she once again took control of her body since being in the ambulance on the way to the ER.

I still wasn't sure what to expect with her waking up, but the doctor knew the exact point when he could start with his response commands. "Cynthia, this is Dr. D," he began reaching for her hands. "Can you squeeze this hand that I am holding?"

We all watched with anticipation like an unexplainable magic trick was being performed. And then the most beautiful thing I've ever observed took place; Cindy responded with the most delicate yet decisive responding squeeze you ever saw. Tears began forming in my eyes. Something so simple can carry so much meaning when it involves the life of a loved one hanging in the balance.

> We all watched with **anticipation** like an unexplainable magic trick was being performed.

"Good job," the doctor encouraged. "Now let's try the other hand. Can you give me a squeeze with that one too?" The response came again as well as the surgeon's affirmation, "Perfect! You are doing really well, Cynthia." The doctor moved down to her feet and gently took hold of Cindy's toes. Wiggling the left toes with his hand, Dr. D asked, "Can you wiggle these toes for me?" The toes responded and moved just as the command requested. He did the same with the right foot and again got a good response. And without waiting a second longer, the doctor motioned to the RN to increase the propofol pump; as quickly as Cindy creaked to life, she lay still once again.

The elation of soul one experiences to see your best friend come to life after a close brush with death is hard to press into the keys of a computer or print onto the pages of a book. And while I was thankful for the simple responses, I felt myself holding back positivity and hope, fearing the damage the swelling of Cindy's brain had caused. I was fearful if Cindy somehow survived this whole ordeal, but did so with quality of life issues, she would never forgive me for allowing her to live. I kept these thoughts to myself and mustered enough emotion to look as though I was thrilled with the response I saw.

As Cindy was rapidly drifting away from the effects of the sedative, Dr. D began his somewhat guarded opinion of what just happened, "Your wife is one of my sickest patients in the hospital, Mr. Wall. When she arrived yesterday, we categorized her at a 5, which is the highest level of criticalness we can give to this type of brain trauma." Not that the scale of severity did anything for my heart and mind, but I did appreciate the fact the doctors were always thorough in their explanations, and they always welcomed questions if presented. "I am truly amazed at what I've seen with Cindy's responses. She presented a little weakness on the right side, but was able to respond to the commands nonetheless. This is a very good sign." He paused momentarily in a typical doctor pose pressing his index finger against his lips and then continued, "But I do want to state with honest caution we have a long way to go. She still needs to be sedated for another 24 hours before we attempt extubating. This will give her continued opportunity for necessary healing. If she pulls through extubating, we'll head into the vasospasm time."

"Vaso what?" I half mumbled to myself, unable to hide my lack of understanding.

The doctor began his explanation of vasospasms and the description reminded me of entering into an enchanted forest similar to the one in a fairy tale, dangerous and unpredictable. The journey would be monitored closely with daily ultrasound diagnostics and medications with the spasms potentially peaking in severity from day five to seven. The danger of vasospasms is the brain will constrict vessels in response to the hemorrhage possibly causing a stroke. So, while there was encouragement with the good response we had seen, we all settled in for a few days of a journey into the unknown.

Once again, the clock in Cindy's room brought its hands to 8 p.m., and it was time to leave the ICU and my best friend again. It was a day of encouragement, but the encouragement was dammed up by a fortified wall of caution preventing us from feeling any relief Cindy was going to recover. We just didn't know at this point.

I began my exit to the door which took me longer than what was necessary. I didn't want to leave, and as I closed the door behind me, the click of the door closing echoed deep into the enchanted forest of vasospasms.

| day 2
born again

Sleep was portioned out to me during the night in much more generous helpings than the night before allowing me to rest so much better. I woke up early before all the others at Maea's and decided to go for a long walk in the cool of the August morning. Spending 12 hours a day in the ICU doesn't do any favors to your physique, so it was great for both body and mind to get out for a brisk walk. My strides were a mix of thoughts, prayers, and of course some tears as I struggled with my natural man in doubt and my spiritual man in faith. I didn't have a plan of how far I was going to walk, and that matched the plan of the day—who knew, but God, what it would bring.

The struggle of trust is fresh every single day in our relationship with God. To me, it seemed my mustard seed faith never grew but always stayed the same. In reality, what grew was the display of God's ability to take all the puzzle pieces of my life and fit them together perfectly. In our tribal language we would say, "Toteyei no 'Alasi lo pelise anititausinokwate," meaning firmly tie or fasten your thoughts to God's Word. Well, with the little strength I had, I was trying to cinch the knot and fasten my heart and mind so I wouldn't fall off the crazy ride I was on.

I made it back to the house at about 7:40 a.m. allowing Essie and me time to stop by the Holiday station for another cup of morning Joe or something that resembled it. Essie grabbed her muffin again, beat me to the till and paid the same smiling lady as the morning before. "I'm buying today!" I stated as the two giggled in delight. "Alright, I'll swallow my pride again," taking a sip of coffee realizing it was a harder swallow than the pride by a long shot.

As we came out of the Holiday station, four police officers had gathered at the side of the building close to where our car was parked. Hoping everything was okay, we approached them and offered to buy them all something to start the morning.

"Hey, officers," I said with a smile, "May we treat you all to coffee and a donut or something?"

Each of the men looked at us in surprise and then exchanged glances with each other. One of them replied for the group, "We're all good, but thanks so much for the offer. We sure appreciate it."

"No problem and thank you all for doing your job. Know that we appreciate and support you all," I said, turning to get in the car.

"Have a great day," they all replied in chorus.

As we got in the car and back in the proper lane to head to the hospital, I said to Essie, "Buying them a cup of this coffee would have been more of an assault on the police than a kind gesture anyway." We shared a laugh, knowing our desire was to show the public servants some support after a summer of turmoil was taking its toll on many wearing the "blue" throughout the country.

At the hospital, we entered the main entrance greeting the valets and the attendants at the check-in desk. Little did they know we would become very familiar with each other over the coming days as each morning we would have to go through all the COVID-19 screening questions and temperature checks before we were issued a new visitor sticker with the current date and room number. This morning's drill made me chuckle as I realized over the past two days we had unknowingly skirted around all protocols by sharing our stickers with each other throughout the day. The poor gals at the desk had no idea who was doing what. Now that the dust had settled a little from the trauma of the first two days, we figured out each person needed to check in and get his own visitor badge.

Entering the room to begin our third day in ICU, it hit me that Cindy had been alone all night. Of course, there was the company of busy nurses in and out all night long doing their all-important monitoring of vitals, pumps and drainage levels, but Cindy was alone without family by her side for an equal 12 hours of time there were visiting hours. The thought made me feel a mixed twinge of disappointment and guilt.

My sad thoughts quickly dissipated as Essie made it to Cindy's bedside. The whole ambiance of the room brightened again as Essie said, "Mom, look what we brought you. Each of the kids made you some artwork to decorate your room." The previous evening, Bryan had opened up the private function room of his restaurant and treated all family and friends to a Mexican dinner buffet. While there, Essie in true organizational fashion had all the kids make art creations for Grammy that could be displayed proudly in her room. Essie continued her explanation and at the same time provided the necessary interpretation of the masterpieces to Cindy. "See here," she held up some samples. "These are shapes of the kids' hands they cut out and signed with their names," Essie explained away, talking as if Cindy wasn't under the influence of propofol and sedated. "Each one says, 'Grammy we love you!'" The presentation was a precious display of all our grandkids' love and affection for their grandma, and under different circumstances, Cindy would have been fawning over each one with an equal measure of love and affection.

"I'll start putting them up on the wall at the foot of the bed and some we'll put on the window so the kids can spot your room from the grass down below," Essie offered to Cindy implementing her plan of action to further brighten and bring life to the room.

Nurse Molly was back on for her third day in a row with Cindy, and it did my heart good to see her again. I knew she wouldn't be assigned to us much longer as she too needed her rest from the intensity of the ICU. She put her hand on my shoulder as I stood looking at Cindy wondering how the day might play out. "How are you doing?" Was the nurse's simple question to me.

"I'm doing ok...considering," was my simple answer which didn't need to be any more complicated than that. I knew Molly didn't need a long explanation or story to frame my state of mind. And while I'm sure she had been through many traumatic and intense situations before, I knew from the touch on my shoulder she carried the perfect blend of professionalism and empathy. She hadn't crossed the line of transference even though she had a connection to our family, but she masterfully came right up to the border of it.

Visitors in and out of the room made the morning pass quickly, and by mid-afternoon, my anxious heart was beating all the more, knowing we were approaching the end of the 48 hours the doctors had asked for. I had made clear if the decision to extubate was made, I wanted, without question, to be in the room. It was great to have family and friends coming by to see Cindy, but under no circumstances was I going to miss that pivotal moment in my life.

The EEG technicians arrived before noon to remove Cindy's beautiful hairdo of wires and electrodes. I have no idea what the 24 hours of monitoring told them, but I figured no news was good news at that point.

Around 3 p.m. I was downstairs enjoying the newly established Wall Family Day Care. Screaming cousins were running to and fro playing freeze tag and soccer with their uncles and dads. I sat at one of the picnic tables enjoying all the activity but also realizing I was exhausted. The intensity of the last two days had drained me of any desire to get up and run with the grandkids or exert any energy to show I wasn't an old grandpa past his ability to break out a few moves on the grass. I'm sure a lot of the reason I just enjoyed watching was the weight of my thoughts as well. They were heavy with the unknown of what the remainder of the day still held.

While I was down having a break, Dr. D arrived at Cindy's room for another response check. Cindy's brother Nate and sister-in-law were currently in the room and got to witness the second creaking to life of Cindy when they backed off the propofol. This time when the doctor felt the sedative had dissipated adequately, he began with the all-important cognitive question of, "What is your name?"

Cindy's brow furrowed as she manifested enough awareness to realize something was down her throat that inhibited her response. Nonetheless, she whispered past the obstruction with a soft, but audible, "Cindy Wall." To Nate, the whisper brought elation to his heart and soul like nothing ever before, confirming her response showed a measure of possibility she might come out of this whole ordeal on the plus side of recovery.

The doctor continued through the rest of the assessment and had the propofol increased to sedate Cindy once again. He turned to the other neurologist with him and had a mini-conference about the decision to extubate. Nate could tell it wasn't an easy decision for them, but the 48-hour mark was within range. Dr. D then said, "What we are seeing is truly amazing. We are only 48 hours in, and the responses are incredible for this stage." No more was said, and the pair of brain surgeons left the room.

It's always hard to measure time in the ICU unless you are making meticulous notes, but somewhere in the following two hours the go-ahead to extubate Cindy was given to nurse Molly and the other RN assisting in the management of room 546.

Essie got the text first from Nate, "Decision made. Will remove life support soon."

"Dad, you need to head up right away," Essie shouted over to me at the other table. "They are going to remove the life support."

I snapped out of my thoughts that had once again carried me far away and wasted no time heading back in the front door of the hospital. Because I had my visitor tag, I bypassed all the entry requirements, and made my way to the elevator, pushed button five and wondered what would greet me at this critical juncture.

Fifth floor ICU was becoming quite familiar to me now, so I sped down the corridor to Cindy's room, making sure I didn't burst through the door in anticipation of what was about to transpire. I opened the blinds from the outside and peered in as other hospital personnel did before entry. It looked okay to me, so I entered and was greeted with great news even though I wasn't sure what it all meant.

"We can tell Cindy is trying to take over the breathing already," Molly stated with confidence in her voice. "We have run her through the spontaneous breathing trial (SBT), and she indicates readiness for liberation."

Liberation? I thought to myself. That's an understatement not knowing the ICU terminology for freeing someone from the ventilator.

"We are ready to give her twenty-five percent control as we begin the liberating process," she continued while monitoring the ventilator computer controlling the apparatus. The other RN worked in tandem monitoring Cindy's mental status (the propofol had already been reduced to zero allowing her to become conscious), oxygenation (to assure breathing on her own provided what the body needed and could absorb for sufficient oxygen levels), ventilation (assuring the breathing was clear), and expectoration (the ability to cough and clear the throat) were all moving in an acceptable direction as the process continued.

I stood with my sister-in-law in amazement as we watched Cindy come to life for literally the third time in a very few short days.

"Twenty-five percent was good; let's move to 50 percent Cindy and 50 percent ventilator," Molly continued as she checked all the observable vitals with her coworker. I didn't have a stopwatch to check the time between each phase of the liberation process, but my racing pulse and surging blood pressure were signs that things were moving quicker than I expected.

"Seventy-five percent Cindy, 25 percent ventilator," was the next thing I comprehended, but I couldn't grasp the significance myself. I had to trust the "pilots" navigating through this landing process with the instruments before them as I had done so many times flying with experts in the jungles of Papua New Guinea. These gals knew what they were doing guiding my wife to the runway of breathing on her own again.

"She is breathing on her own," Molly said, turning to me with the most reassuring smile I had ever seen. "She's in control 100 percent now."

My heart and soul were completely overwhelmed. The rising and falling of my beautiful wife's frame were being generated by her own ability to breathe again and not a machine doing it for her. Instantly, I thought, *Can she continue doing the work?* I know that's silly, but it hits you that way. That miracle of breath. I'd never look at the involuntary breathing of the human body the same again. What a function. What a design.

Within a few short minutes, extubating the breathing apparatus began. The best way to describe it is the birth of a child, when she takes her first breath on the outside of the womb. The parents wait in great anticipation as there is the initial cough and sputter and then the exhilarating burst of crying as the little one begins life on her own. When Cindy's tube was removed, I edged closer to her bed with fists clenched and cheering, "Breathe, honey! Breathe!" The cough and the sputter sounded, and once again I heard the beautiful music of my wife breathing on her own again.

> I edged closer to her bed with fists clenched and cheering, "Breathe, honey! Breathe!"

Her eyes tried to open in the discomfort of what she just went through. They were large and saggy like giant dark grapes, watered by tear ducts that hadn't been used in several days, but they were beautiful to see. Her head was free to move upon release of the apparatus that had locked her in place the last two days and she slowly turned to look in my direction. Her focus was blurred, and I'm sure she had no idea where she was and how she got there, but the tiny effort to orientate to her surroundings was evidence of a huge step in the direction of recovery for those of us surrounding the bed.

The exhaustion and fatigue that accompany a traumatic brain injury are extreme, and in all our thrill and excitement to see Cindy on the living side of this whole ordeal, we had to carefully measure the amount of stimulation and interaction we so desired to offer her. One small vessel in her brain had hemorrhaged, yet the effect was body-wide. The central control for every thought, movement and function had taken a hit causing everything to suffer the loss of energy and stamina. We would learn quickly over the next few days how much Cindy could handle our unending family support and how it would have to fit in around life in the ICU.

Toward evening two new nurses came into the room to get their briefing from Molly for the change of shift. Molly was thorough in her update as to how Cindy was doing and gave special instructions for the drain setup and monitoring of the discharge of fluid. As she was finishing up and ready to leave, I made my way over to her. "Well, I'll be back in the morning for one last shift with you guys and then I'm off for a few days of much needed rest," she offered before I could speak.

"Actually," I said, dragging the word out as long as I could while trying not to let her see any expression of jest on my face, "I've talked with your superiors and got the ok to have you on shift the entire duration of Cindy's stay in ICU."

Her eyes widened, but then I couldn't contain my joking smile. "Molly, you have been amazing these past three days, and I want you to know my family and I felt the utmost confidence in your ability to care for Cindy. So, thank you from our entire family."

I could see from her response the expression of gratitude touched her heart and she responded, "It's been my privilege, and please know your family is amazing, and your support for her will contribute greatly to her recovery." And with that, she ended her second to last shift in ICU with us.

I turned back to my sleeping wife and enjoyed the sound of life breathing on its own accord. Once again, the clock snuck up behind me without a noise and indicated it was time to leave; I gave Cindy a light parting kiss on the forehead, whispered, "I love you" and left for the evening.

| day 3
a hundred times

Sleep was coming easier each evening. I wasn't sure if it was from a heart at peace because of Cindy coming through the events of the past few days or because I was simply exhausted. A combination of both I imagine. Nonetheless, I was thankful that rest was coming easier.

Essie and I got ready first to head over to the hospital, but this morning we elected not to stop at the gas station. As much as I wanted to show off to the kind old lady at the till and have her witness my daughter buying my coffee again, I couldn't pull myself to suffer through another cup of that sorry excuse for morning Joe. I would have to find another source for my morning inspiration, and it came later in the morning from Jordan's wife Charissa. She brought me the most amazing home-brewed coffee I had ever had. The flavor was rich and satisfying. At that point, my mornings became something to look forward to again.

We arrived at the front desk and went through our screening with the gals who were now recognizing us as regulars. "It looks as though we'll get to see your smiling faces for another three weeks," I commented as I checked in and slapped on my visitor's badge. "My wife pulled through the critical stage and is off life support."

"That's wonderful!" The ladies said in chorus. "We trust she'll have a speedy recovery," they offered as we made our way to the elevators.

"Thanks! And you both have a great day because it is a great day," I said, hoping to shine a little ray of sunshine into their lives in a place where too many people come and go with difficult burdens. Maybe God could use us to bring some cheer from the hope we had in us.

We got to the room expecting a calmer atmosphere now that Cindy was off life support and breathing on her own. But, as I cracked the door open, I was shocked to see the TV was on with some home improvement show. I was a little confused at first because Cindy doesn't watch TV unless she's pretty much forced to...by me. I wondered what was going on. How could she be up to watching TV already when under normal circumstances, she doesn't? I also noticed a gal sitting on the opposite side of the room, who was apparently enjoying the program displayed on the wall-mounted unit.

"Good morning," I said as politely as possible without consideration for the show. "My wife doesn't watch TV. Like ever." I stated calmly and then requested, "May I have it turned off... permanently?"

"Oh, no problem." The response came in a thick West African accent that piqued my interest.

Just as I was about to ask the gal where she was from, Molly came in the door and took my attention. "Good morning," she said with enthusiasm as she had just begun her shift an hour earlier and had plenty of energy for the next 12 hours or so. "Looks like Cindy got a little aggressive on us during the night."

"What do you mean?" I asked curiously.

"In my briefing from the night shift RN's, they said she was pretty agitated and began pulling out IVs and anything she could get her hands on. Thankfully one of the nurses showed up as she was trying to figure out the

EVD attached to her head," she said with a look of "that would've been bad."

"Are you serious?" I asked, looking back at what I thought was my peaceful wife too tired and exhausted to lift a hand.

"So the RN's got everything reattached and set properly, but they did secure her arms with the restraints until we could get an attendant to watch her," Molly explained. "And the attendants will be in place 24/7 for the duration of her stay in ICU."

Essie and I both looked at each other not knowing if we should burst out laughing or not. I knew my wife, and Essie knew her mom, and her feistiness didn't surprise either one of us. And then it hit why the TV was on when I came in; the poor CNA had to sit there all night and somehow stay awake and do her job monitoring her agitated patient's attempt to remove anything touching her body. I had a twinge of empathy in my heart for the gal, but I didn't renege on the instructions to leave the TV turned off.

"Are we allowed to wake her?" Essie asked the nurse politely, hoping to interact with her mom.

"That's no problem if she's up to it," she said with a smile. "You'll just have to be careful not to overstimulate her at this point in recovery. But you'll figure out what she can handle as her fatigue will be extreme these initial days."

"Yeah, I see what you're saying," Essie agreed, turning to her mom and putting her hand on her face in the gentlest way possible. "Hey, Mom. It's Essie. Dad and I are back for a visit," she announced in a gentle yet crisp voice.

Cindy's eyes opened slowly like mechanical shades on a pair of large office windows as she lay on her right side in her bed of four days. Her eyes were heavy and showed exhaustion but were much clearer than the day before following her extubation. A slight smile broke across her mouth matching the speed of her eyes opening. "Hi, honey," she whispered, acknowledging Essie's greeting. The sight was absolutely beautiful considering all she'd been through. And a cognitive response was definitely a gift Essie received with delight.

"Mom, is it okay if I sing with you for a bit to start the day?" Essie asked as Cindy's eyelids were slowly making their way down to the closed position again.

"Sure," came the soft and extended response. And so began the beautiful sound of Essie's voice singing choruses and hymns that Cindy knew so well. As a special treat, Essie also pulled out some tribal worship songs from the recesses of her memory of growing up in a tribe. I beamed with pride. Cindy cracked a slight smile when she heard the tribal language and even the CNA perked up in curiosity, as she was from Liberia and felt a connection.

The room filled with a pleasant ambiance of singing and scripture reading as we got as close alongside Cindy as possible. As long as we were right by the bed's edge, we could put the railings down, inch in and maintain contact so she could feel our love and presence.

Just as we settled in for what we thought was the restful road to recovery, the door opened, and two technicians entered. They pulled a monitor on a rolling cart with numerous squirt bottles lining its sides. "Sorry to bother you, but we are ultrasound, and we are here for the morning's doppler test," one of the technicians announced politely without asking permission to take over the room. Essie and I backed up from the side of the bed and made room for the technicians to do their thing.

"So what exactly does the doppler test do?" I asked out of curiosity, not wanting to show my surprise at being interrupted while visiting my wife.

The techs were more than happy to explain and so began, "The doppler ultrasound is a test that uses high-frequency sound waves to measure the amount of blood flowing through the patient's veins supplying blood to the head. Vascular analysis can detect abnormal flow within a blood vessel."

"Okay," I said slowly nodding my head with my new knowledge. I knew they used ultrasound for pregnancies as Facebook makes abundantly clear on a daily basis, but also for measuring vascular activity? "How often will you do testing for Cindy?" I inquired.

"Every morning at this time," the tech replied without breaking stride as he set equipment up to begin the test. "The test only takes about half an hour, so not long at all," he concluded, now focused completely on the readings beginning to show on the monitor. The techs began at the temple on one side of Cindy's head and worked their way around to the other side to complete the test. I was glad they didn't leave a goopy trail of the gel after each stop on their journey past all the vessels they were checking, but they did leave a blue mark in Cindy's hair on both sides of her head marking the start and finish of their analysis.

The ultrasound techs finished up their test and rolled out of the room just as they had rolled in. I was afraid to ask any more questions about what they had observed, figuring no news was good news. I was sure a doctor in some other part of the hospital would analyze the readings anyway. Essie and I moved in close to Cindy and again resumed our quiet visit with her. I pulled out my phone and began reading in 2 Corinthians to continue what would be our normal morning practice at home. Just a couple of verses in, the door opened again. It was nurse Molly.

"We need to do a response check again," she announced in her non-autocratic yet take-control and get-the-job-done kind of way. "Every hour on the hour we've been waking Cindy to make sure her responses are tracking well."

Once again, we backed up and let the professionals take over. "Cindy!" Molly began, surprising me at how loud she talked to Cindy. "I want you to wake up for a little bit and answer some questions for me." Cindy began to stir a little as Molly turned back to us and said in a quieter voice, "We've been doing these checks since the middle of the night."

Seeing that Cindy was having a hard time waking up, Molly rubbed the top of her sternum to help the process.

"Cindy, what is your name?" Molly asked, back in her accentuated tone for Cindy to hear.

"Cindy Wall," the response came from Cindy's whispering lips.

"Good. Good," Molly affirmed. "How old are you?"

"Fifty-five." Another right answer came out.

"What month is it?" Molly asked.

There was a little hesitation, but then the answer came, "August, I think."

"Where are you right now?" Molly asked for orientation clarity.

"In Bemidji."

"Actually, you're in Fargo." Molly corrected gently and then queried further. "What kind of building are you in?"

Cindy pursed her lips outward as she thought of her location, "A hospital."

"Very good," Molly affirmed as she moved to check Cindy's ability to squeeze with her hands, wiggle her toes and even lift her legs. "Excellent," Molly concluded. "You've done a great job, Cindy."

But Cindy was already back asleep; she'd had enough activity for the hour.

As Molly went over to the room's computer I followed and said, "Molly, she now knows she's in the hospital in Fargo, but please don't tell her why she's here yet. I want to do that." I knew Cindy wouldn't be happy with me when she found out she'd had an aneurysm just like her mother and survived. It's not that she didn't want to live, by any stretch of the imagination; she was just ready to meet her Savior. In the right way, if Cindy passed away as her mother had, it would be an honor so to speak. Added to that, her mother didn't suffer or experience a diminished quality of life. Cindy's mom was a very active woman, always serving others. It would have been difficult for her if she had survived, only to live with paralysis or diminished mental capacity. I didn't explain all this to Molly in detail, but I did conclude, "When she's ready, I'll explain the whole situation to her and what happened in detail. Otherwise, I might be the one in ICU."

The room turned quiet again, and we moved closer to Cindy's bedside. No singing or scripture for now. Cindy, we could see, was worn out by the morning's interactions. Her energy reserves were limited and she succumbed to exhaustion as if settling under a heavy blanket in the depth of winter. There was no need to push her. We were in the ICU for the long haul, and rest was exactly what she needed to help her recover.

Extended family and friends gathered at the picnic tables, so we began the revolving door of alloted visitors for the day. Each one was given strict instructions not to wake Cindy unnecessarily as she needed to sleep. Every hour when she'd be roused for response checks, the guests could sneak in little visits with her.

By midafternoon I was back in the room when yet another technician showed up.

"Good afternoon," the pleasant and soft-spoken gentleman greeted as he came into the room. "I'm with physiotherapy, and I'd like to start Cindy on some exercises if I may."

The therapist looked pretty advanced in years and reminded me of my dear French teacher from high school, Mr. Peterson, one of the gentlest people on this earth. But that was 35 years ago, and Mr. Peterson is now in his 90's. As that thought quickly passed, another rushed in, "PT already? Are you kidding? She can hardly move, and they want her up exercising?"

The therapist must have read my thoughts, about as subtle as a highway billboard and quickly explained, "Obviously, this PT session will be rather simple with the goal of at least getting Cynthia to sit up on the side of the bed. No walking or anything else, just sitting up will be the goal." And with that, he gently asked Cindy if she could wake up while beginning to move her legs.

Cindy stirred a little as she struggled from under that blanket of exhaustion. She didn't actually open her eyes, but the therapist began anyway.

"Cynthia, can you help me lift your leg?" He gently requisitioned while assisting Cindy with the motion. "That's it. Now help me by pulling your knee toward your chest."

To me, it looked like Cindy slipped back under the heavy blanket again, but the therapist kept stimulating her to the best of his ability. I was so impressed with how gentle he was and made a mental note to ask him if he spoke French by any chance.

"Ok, keep working with me, Cynthia. Let's move your leg outward and do some rotations for those hips," the therapist continued, fully knowing Cindy was drifting slowly in and out of the deep sleep that had a stronger hold on her than his grip on her leg. "Good job," he affirmed. "Let's move to the other leg and do the same sort of motions." As he moved to her left leg, he looked at me with a pleasant smile as he began sliding her left leg out from the sheets. "Not a whole lot of help from her at this point, but it's still important to get the joints moving even if I'm doing all the work," he explained.

"Yeah, looks like she's not quite ready to wake up yet," I concurred.

"That's okay," the kind man assured. "I think we'll skip the sitting up part; we can try for that tomorrow instead. She's definitely a little too groggy to push her that far." So the kind therapist wrapped up his session and moved on to the next room down the hall. I thanked him as he left, resisting the urge to say, "Merci Beaucoup" in French.

We let Cindy have the sleep her body craved, but before long it was time for another response check. I wondered how she could ever rest given the constant stream of medical personnel in and out of the room. I simply had to resign myself to the fact they knew what they were doing.

It was nurse Molly's last check on Cindy before she was off for a few well-deserved days of rest. She came into the room focused on her task, leaning over to Cindy, and said in a not-so-quiet voice, "Cindy, can you wake up for me?" Cindy wasn't wanting to wake up to another round of answering questions, squeezing and wiggling her toes, but Molly wasn't giving her the option to sleep. "Cindy!" she said louder as she rubbed the top of Cindy's sternum again to stimulate her. "I need to ask you a few questions."

Cindy's head moved slightly as her brow turned into a slight frown indicating she was trying to climb out of her deep sleep. She pursed her lips and swallowed before saying, "Okay," in a light whisper.

"Cindy, what is your full name?" Molly began again as I thought Cindy would never forget this process.

"Cindy Wall," came the soft reply.

"What is your birthdate?" Molly continued the regimen of questions.

There was a slight pause before the answer made its way out of her lips, but not wanting to lead the way out of her slumber, "April 1st, 1965."

"Good," Molly encouraged bringing the decibels down a slight notch below the safety level of 85. "And what month is it today?"

You could see Cindy was working to remember the answers to the questions even though she'd already been asked them many times in the last 24 hours since she was extubated. "August," came the answer with a strengthened exhale.

"Very good and where are you currently?" the nurse asked.

I could see the questions were purposely ordered to orientate Cindy as much as possible. In previous questioning, she kept thinking she was back in Bemidji, but this time I could see the gears of her mind turning to come up with the correct answer. She turned her head slowly in my direction and said from behind closed eyes, "Fargo. In the hospital in Fargo."

"That's exactly right," Molly affirmed. It was such a simple and little accomplishment, but huge on the cognitive scale as Cindy was now realizing where she was. I expected Molly to finish the Q&A, but to my surprise, she had one more question, a new question.

"Cindy, do you know why you are here?" Molly asked. My systolic blood pressure skyrocketed and instantly topped the 200 mark they were keeping Cindy under. What did I just hear Molly ask? I was gobsmacked. I wanted that explanation, the story of her journey, to come from me. I didn't want her to be mad at me for the rest of whatever life she was going to salvage out of this whole ordeal. I stood there gaping, unable to intervene.

In response, Cindy shook her head slightly and whispered, "I dunno."

I drew a breath to bring down my panic, hoping Molly would leave it there, but she continued.

"Cindy, you've had a brain aneurysm just like your mother," Molly stated without hesitation.

Cindy's head was already positioned in my direction and no sooner had Molly's words left her lips than Cindy's eyes popped open and locked onto mine with daggers. It was just a moment and clearly took all her energy. But it was enough. That look seared into me, and I felt that depth of her being ready to hold me accountable. No words needed.

Guilty to the core. I had some explaining to do. Cindy knew exactly what the nurse had said, and her reaction was nothing less than I expected.

> Cindy's eyes popped open and **locked onto mine** with daggers.

When Molly had finished the hand squeezes and toe wiggles, I politely asked her to step into the hall for a word. "Molly," I began maintaining my composure under a few shades of red from the spike in blood pressure. "I wanted to tell Cindy why she was here. Did you see the daggers that came out of those eyes?"

Molly was understanding, yet professional, "Yes, I saw them. But she needed to know the reason for being here sooner than later."

I could see the nurse was firm in her professional position and therefore I backed down. "Well, it'll be a while before I tell her the whole story, but if she doesn't come through this 100 percent, I'm in trouble."

I went back into the room and found Cindy sound asleep, as she had easily surrendered to her exhaustion. I stayed with her, imagining how I would tell this story and how she would respond to the fact her life had been saved multiple times in the last several days. Cindy was not afraid to die, but she also did not want extreme measures taken only to diminish the quality of her life. I had one advantage to spare me for now. Cindy's memory was extremely short at this point in the recovery. Yes, she could remember the response questions, but she had no recollection of anything during those initial days. Nonetheless, I began rehearsing my lines in anticipation of the time when she was rested and coherent enough to hear the whole story.

It was time to switch out for other visitors. I made sure to manage times closely so I could have the last hour or so with Cindy before the day ended.

As usual, the day passed quickly. But this time we hit a new milestone as Cindy followed me with her eyes all the way to the door. I could see the effort it took to do such a simple thing, but she was determined to see me to the door in the only way her weary body would allow. When I got to the door I mouthed, "I love you."

She returned, "I love you" back with those beautiful lips I know only too well.

I couldn't leave and rushed back to her side. Pressing gently against her with as much of me as possible, I whispered softly in her ear, "Honey, I would marry you a hundred times again."

With eyes now closed having spent her limited energy tracking me, she cracked a cornered smile in approval, "I love you too."

I backed out the door, drinking in her gaze that followed me once again. I gave a final gentle wave as I stood halfway across the threshold. And in return, Cindy raised her weaker right arm to "wave" goodbye.

The whole Wall crew with spouses and children.

Nearly 60 hours on life support.

Our daughter Essie singing and reading scripture to her mom.

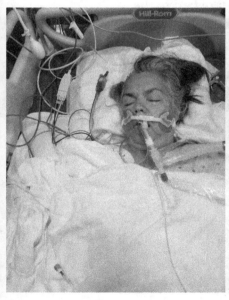

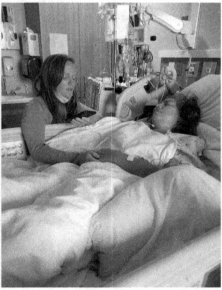

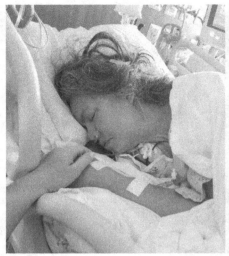
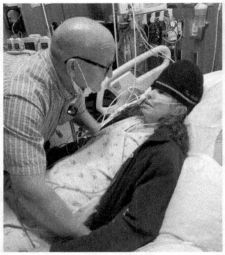

It's incredible how brain trauma takes everything you have and more.

A clean shave to surprise Cindy while she's sporting the Tim Horton's toque.

First journey out of bed to the chair and then back to the bed.

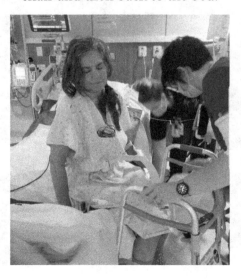

Cindy was determined to walk as much as possible, with help of course. Pictured here with Jordan and Maea.

Cindy loves her littles.

| day 4
nuggets

Day four. Extreme fatigue was obvious. Cindy loved seeing us come through the doors but greeted us with only a soft smile. The ICU is not a place of rest by any stretch of the imagination. The day was already busy with lots of doctors, nurses, therapists and CNA'S checking in to track Cindy's progress. The doppler crew showed up right on time to perform the vascular ultrasound and re-ink the blue marks on the side of Cindy's head. They gathered their information and were off again to the next stop on their rounds.

Two female physical therapists arrived at the door to work with Cindy and get her joints moving again. The lead PT was pleasant, but I was pretty sure she played right guard in college football. The pair politely woke Cindy and began asking her to move her legs and do some exercises while still lying on the bed. Their interactions were affirming yet intentional in having Cindy move as much as was possible.

Part of the way into the simple session Cindy whispered, "I'd like to brush my teeth." After several days of not eating, we didn't have to tell her she needed to brush her teeth; she knew very well hospital breath is akin to breath found in the trenches of WWI.

"That would be just fine for you to do," the lead PT agreed with excitement. "But we'll need to sit you up. Maybe even have you sit in that chair."

"Sure," came the response from Cindy without any voluntary effort to move toward the chair.

"Ok, we'll have to put a belt around you first to assist in helping you get from the bed to the chair. It's a little cumbersome but helps secure you and us," the PT informed politely. The second PT knew exactly what to do and reached for the gait belt hanging over the sharps box attached to the wall of the room. The pair worked to sit Cindy upright at the edge of the bed and then secured the belt in place around her waist. At the same time an RN monitored and controlled the EVD making sure it was turned off, so no excess fluid drained as Cindy sat up. The process was beginning to resemble the construction of a highrise building in downtown New York—with human cranes, coordination of workers and fitting parts and pieces into place. The CNA grabbed the urinary catheter drain line and retention container to give Cindy enough tether to make it to the chair. Other leads and IV lines were all moved accordingly, a snail's pace rigmarole that got Cindy sitting in the chair. I stood by in awe of the complex coordination required to accomplish the task.

It was the first time Cindy sat up in a chair in several days. My elation quickly gave way as I could see Cindy was painfully uncomfortable. The pressure in her head was one thing, but even worse was the pain and discomfort her muscle and skeletal structure were feeling. Nonetheless, the goal was to sit up and get the pearly whites brushed.

"Here you go, Cynthia," one of the PT's said, down on one knee beside Cindy and offering a hospital-issued toothbrush with a swatch of toothpaste on it. "Do you want me to brush your teeth or would you like me to help you?"

"I'll try myself," she responded as one having just run a full marathon from the edge of the bed to the chair. Cindy slowly took hold of the brush, managed to direct it slowly into her mouth and began brushing. The whole process unfolded at the speed of a flower opening to the sunshine after a night of rest. You can't actually see the flower open; you have to turn away for a time, look again, then see the progress. Nonetheless, Cindy was able to brush her teeth and enjoy the feeling of clean teeth once again.

When done with the brushing, Cindy indicated the chair was too uncomfortable to sit in any longer and requested transitioning back to the bed. So the whole coordination process of the RN's, PT's and CNA's went in reverse order, settling Cindy back into her bed, where she fell back into a deep sleep completely exhausted by her first excursion from it.

I so much appreciated the patience and care the crew offered to Cindy. Something as simple as getting out of bed to sit in a chair was now a complicated procedure taking many skillful hands to accomplish. But each one on the team did her job with great care.

The rest of the morning included a rotation of visitors, response evaluations and a little applesauce sent up from the kitchen by the dietitian. It was time for Cindy to start eating a little more, beginning with a diet of soft foods only.

Midafternoon yet another discipline showed up, Occupational Therapy. A short bouncy personality of a gal introduced herself and explained she was there to begin Cindy's OT. Now I wasn't sure of the difference between OT and PT, but the therapist was more than willing to give an explanation. Like all the other hospital staff, she explained things with care so her patient's loved ones could understand. Physical therapy, I learned, focuses on gross motor function, while occupational therapy focuses on how the patient uses fine motor and cognitive skills to perform tasks that are meaningful to them.

"So this is perfect timing," the OT began, "Cindy's ready to begin eating, so we can help her with those necessary motor skills that might be challenged as a result of her brain trauma."

"Wow, I'm slightly blown away by all the care we are receiving and the coordination it takes to provide it," I said in a long exhale of appreciation. "I would have never imagined all this goes into helping someone recover."

"We love to see progress," the OT said. "Sometimes it's slow, but if we begin as soon as possible, it helps the patient recover better with those little, but essential skills to live a normal life," she concluded.

"So true," I agreed while hoping and praying on the inside Cindy would get all those skills back.

Over the course of the afternoon, the sanctioned grandkids outside at the daycare command center were able to FaceTime with Grammy in between her sleeps. It took a lot of energy for Cindy to do so as screen time stimulation is exhausting. But you could see the interaction with the littles filled her veins with joy even as the other three IV lines hooked into her were pumping meds and saline into her system.

When she finished with the kiddos, my phone began buzzing again with another video call—from Australia. My heart leaped with excitement as I swept the arrow up accepting Seth's call. "Seth!" I said, trying to hold the phone still as I shook with emotion. "This is perfect timing to call. Mom's right here and awake," I explained. The coordination of talking with loved ones on the other side of the world and the international date line is complicated in the best of times, but here were Seth, Emily, Eva and Manila framed into the screen of my phone looking at their mom and Grammy.

Cindy's heart was thrilled, and the smile on her face was fueled by the tiny reserve of energy she had to spare.

"Grammy, I'm drawing a picture for you," Eva piped in right away.

The gesture was precious, and Cindy responded without hesitation, "I look forward to getting that. Thank you, Eva."

The interaction that followed was great medicine for Cindy, but also for Seth and his family as they were on the tail end of their two-week quarantine in downtown Sydney, Australia. The chance to see their mom and grandma gave great reprieve from being confined to the 23rd floor apartment they had been in for so long. It did all our hearts good.

Toward evening Essie and I were talking about friends of hers in Florida who wanted to help our family in a practical way. They ordered Chick-fil-A for the whole group of 16 of us. The gesture was beyond anything we could imagine and gave a whole new meaning to long-distance takeout. As Essie continued to explain the connection she had with her friends, we both assumed Cindy was sleeping and disengaged from our excitement and anticipation of having tender chicken nuggets with all the fixings for supper. But then, we heard a quiet, "Honey."

> **"I want chicken,"** came the demand again now dipped in Chick-fil-A certainty sauce.

I leaned over closer and replied, "Yes, what is it?"

"I want chicken," the quiet yet direct request followed.

Startled, I countered with a chuckle of doubt, "Sweetheart, you're on a special diet. The nurses won't allow that."

"I want chicken," came the demand again, now dipped in Chick-fil-A certainty sauce.

I looked over at the nurse busily typing notes at the room's computer station. "I'll check with the nurses and see what I can do," knowing there was no way they'd agree to break the pureed diet that had been making its way up from the kitchen gallows below.

I walked over to the other side of the room and, with an apologetic half-smile on my face, said to the RN, "I guess Cindy was eavesdropping on our conversation about chicken nuggets and now thinks she'd like to eat some." There was no attempt to ask permission on my part. I didn't want to appear naïve with such a request this early in the game.

"Oh, that'd be fine," the nurse responded without missing a keystroke, "Her gag reflux since extubating seems to be a non-issue."

"Ahhh, so you're saying she can have some chicken nuggets?" I responded with some doubt, certain she wouldn't be allowed such a delicacy. "Like this is Chick-fil-A we're talking about, not pablum out of a jar with a picture of a chicken on it," I added to further clarify hoping not to insult the intelligence of an ICU nurse tasked with overseeing the wellbeing of a patient who recently returned from death's door.

"As long as the pieces are cut up nice and small and she eats slowly, she should be fine," came the affirmative response without breaking stride in her notes flowing from her fingertips.

In total surprise, I pivoted on the ball of my foot and declared, "Bring up the nuggets!" I'm sure the declaration could have been heard all the way down to the kitchen where the dietician was deciding on the next round of nutrients to throw in the blender. But I didn't care, my wife wanted chicken nuggets, and chicken nuggets she was gonna get. A slight smile of pleasure broke out across Cindy's face confirming her delight that Chick-fil-A was now on order.

Essie texted down to the family daycare where the feeding had already commenced compliments of the kind Floridian friends, "Grammy wants chicken. Bring up nuggets ASAP!"

The text was read aloud down below, and the noise of the makeshift fast-food eatery came to an instant standstill. "Grammy wants chicken!" Jordan announced. "ASAP!" Focus suddenly changed from caring for the toddlers and dipping sauce to getting an order ready to be couriered up to room 546. It was a simple task, but the care and delight that went into the operation were fueled by the fact that Grammy wanted chicken. And that showed she was definitely headed in the direction of recovery.

The last hour of the day showed up again, and I found myself posted alongside Cindy's bed watching her rest after all the excitement of having her tiny yet monumental order of chicken nuggets. My thoughts filled my mind with encouragement and some doubt as I considered the next few days at the edge of the enchanted forest of vasospasms. It almost seemed easier to trust God with the dire predicament we faced during life support than face the unknown of possible stroke during the next 72 hours.

| day 5
pain tolerance

When I left last evening, I had a sense Cindy was uncomfortable, and this morning it was confirmed. Cindy's natural pain tolerance is high, so when she complains about pain, you know it's bad. Back about eight years ago, Cindy began mentioning, not complaining, about a dull pain in her mid- to lower back. I wondered if it wasn't the onset of kidney stones that she had experienced the last year we were in Papua New Guinea. Several days into not feeling right, Cindy woke me up in the middle of the night and said, "The pain is really bad right now, and it's moved around to the front of my abdomen."

It was now quite evident Cindy was in acute pain and uncomfortable. "Honey, we better go to the ER. You've got me worried now." She agreed, so we began getting ready for the drive into the hospital. I woke the three younger kids still at home with us to let them know I was taking their mom in, and we'd be back as soon as possible.

At the ER the doctor came into the waiting room still looking fresh even though it was early morning. "How can we help you this fine morning?" He asked with a comforting amount of cheer for us both.

Overcome with pain, Cindy couldn't answer, so I filled the doctor in on the situation and a bit of history. "She's been experiencing some back pain in the kidney area for a couple days, and now it's moved to the front right side of her abdomen, and it's become acute, as you can see," I began for the doctor.

Without any visible reaction, he began to examine Cindy and immediately concluded, "I'd like to order a CT scan and get a good look at what's going on in there." And with that Cindy was wheeled off to another part of the hospital. I had no time to respond as the doctor knew something was up and took no time to discuss options.

In record time, less than 30 minutes, the doctor was back. "Your wife has a ruptured appendix, and her entire abdomen is filled with infection and toxins," he stated in a serious voice. "We're taking her into surgery right away."

"What?" I responded in shock. "Appendicitis is the easiest thing on earth to access," I continued with a look of disbelief on my face. "Three of us in the family have already had it. That's crazy because the pain started in the back two days ago and only this morning did it present in the front where appendicitis usually manifests."

The doctor let me vent a little, but then added, "If she didn't manifest acute pain until this morning, that's some incredible pain tolerance."

"Yeah, she does have that," I agreed. "She had an unnaturally easy time delivering each of our kids compared to what some women go through."

"Alright, we'll get the procedure going and be in touch post-op," the doctor assured as he disappeared through the large door leading back into the restricted area of the hospital.

As it turned out, Cindy spent six days in the hospital to clear the infection. And all because of a pain tolerance that is like none other.

So now as I stood beside Cindy, she was complaining about cramping in her thighs, and I knew it meant the pain was intense. She figured it was varicose veins, but the pain wasn't in her lower legs, but in her thighs. Nonetheless, if she was complaining, it had to be intense. As visitors began to come to the room, we had each one take a turn massaging the back of her thighs to help as much as possible to relieve the discomfort.

In discussion with the nurses about what was causing the cramping, I learned the blood from the hemorrhage that didn't drain out through the EVD was now being absorbed by the brain into the cerebrospinal fluid or CSF and being disbursed through the body. The pain or cramping of the thighs in all likelihood was due to this phenomenon. Unfortunately for Cindy, this pain was going to be part of her recovery for many days to come. It was hard to watch her struggle with the discomfort of the cramps that seemed to come in waves. There were options for stronger pain management available to us, but we decided to stick with the non-narcotic-based options like Tylenol and Ibuprofen on a rotational basis.

Another issue Cindy had to deal with was being cold. We adjusted the room temperature, but then everyone else who entered the room felt uncomfortably warm. Of course, she was the priority as the patient, but eventually, we resorted to warm blankets that were changed out regularly. And because she couldn't warm up, she began insisting I crawl into bed with her. I would gently decline and remind her I wasn't allowed to climb into bed with all the gear she was hooked up to.

A bright spot came later in the day when we somehow convinced the nurses to allow us to bring Addy up to the room to see Grammy. In my mind, this was another milestone in the recovery process for Cindy, so I was emphatic that I be the one to take the little visitor in to see her.

Chas and Lexi prepared their five year old as best they could for the visit up to room 546. As we were about ready to go, I bent down to ask,

"Sweetheart, are you ready to go see Grammy?"

Her deep brown eyes locked with mine and her sweet little voice responded with determined bravery, "I'm ready Bubby."

I was already beginning to choke up as I took her little hand in mine, and we made our way to the glass door entrance of the hospital. It made me so proud to escort the special visitor with her kid-sized mask in place and her beautiful brown hair bouncing alongside with each stride we took. Once inside we made sure the ladies at the desk were aware we had permission to head up to the ICU. We continued to the elevators making sure Addy got to push the "Up" button to summon the elevator for our ascent to the ICU ward. After a short wait, our lift arrived.

"Can you find button number five?" I asked, making sure Addy had as much opportunity to make this journey her own.

"Sure," came her confident response as she took only a second to point to the button. "That's how old I am."

"Go ahead and push it," I gently instructed. "That'll take us all the way up to Grammy's floor where she's resting."

When we arrived at the room, I opened the blinds on the door again to make sure there was no activity going on. I hoped Cindy was just resting so we could make this visit as special as possible for both her and Addy. It looked like the coast was clear, so we quietly entered the room.

I was trying to maintain my composure the best I could, but I'm sure my mask was soaked with tears by this point. Addy maintained her composure much better as her eyes zeroed in on Cindy lying before her. Cindy's position in the bed was perfect as she had turned on her side and was facing us as we entered. She was in a deep sleep, enjoying some relief from the cramping that had become her main visitor of late.

There were no nurses in the room except the CNA who was on the other side of the bed, so I grabbed the taller office chair at the nurses' computer station for Addy. With a quick press of the lever on the side, the seat shot up to the tallest height perfect for Addy to scoot right in close to her grammy.

As I moved Addy up close alongside the bed, I whispered one final instruction, "You can go ahead and wake Grammy up; she would love to visit with you."

"Ok," the whisper of affirmation came as Addy leaned in and began to gently rub Cindy's hand that was partially wedged in at the side of her peaceful face.

"Grammy," the tender little voice began without any instruction as her mature five-year-old intuition took control. "It's Addy, I'm here to visit you."

Cindy's eyes opened slowly from her rest and instantly showed delight in whom she saw. She rolled her hand over and took hold of Addy's little hand reuniting the pair in what had seemed like an eternity of separation from each other.

> The words could have **melted** the hardest heart of steel anywhere in the universe.

Addy knew her next line without any training, preparation or instruction, "I love you, Grammy." The words could have melted the hardest heart of steel anywhere in the universe. I looked on through a cascade of tears. My heart began to heal and mend in the presence of all that love in Room 546.

The two had a little visit together after which I took time to explain all the wires and lines hooked up to Grammy. I also led Addy to the window to have her look down to where she and the other grandkids would come to wave to whoever was visiting in the room at any particular time.

Unfortunately, the short time the nurses graciously allowed for Addy's visit came to an end, and she had to leave her Grammy's side. But the visit had done both of them so much good, the healing afforded to Cindy by seeing her granddaughter and the joy of young Addy knowing that her visit meant so much to her Grammy.

As we neared the end of day five, we were all encouraged that the first day into the enchanted forest of vasospasms passed without incident. Two days to go.

The doctors had begun to move Cindy from IV to oral medications. They were hard pills to swallow at first because of the size—real horse pills, especially the one called Nimotop for the vasospasm control. Cindy also began feeding herself, a sometimes slow and tedious process, but one more step toward independence.

With just an hour left for visiting, Cindy whispered another attempt to get me to lie down beside her in bed. She could sense my hesitation and managed a couple of ounces of sternness in her voice as she justified the request, "Who cares about all this stuff; your lying beside me will make me better."

Trying not to sound uncaring and recovering from the dagger of love she plunged into my heart, I replied, "Honey, you are still in critical condition, so the nurses won't allow it."

She responded by slowly lifting her arms, settling for a hug as a distant second best. I bent over the bed rail cautiously paying attention to her "brain drain" as we called it and gave her a light hug. I could tell she drank in every amount of physical touch. And then I felt it, she was nibbling on my ear!

"You are so bad," I whispered as loudly as I could all the while making sure I didn't knock over any critical care equipment!

I didn't want to tell Cindy at that moment I was going back to Bemidji in the morning, because her short-term memory was challenged at this point in the recovery. But I did have a sense as we embraced it was time to tell her the story of why she was in the hospital. Of course, she knew the answer as to why she was in the hospital when they asked the regiment of response questions every hour. But I still hadn't explained the actual story of what had happened to her.

The time was right. I needed to tell her what took us down this path. It was clear to me that God Himself had brought us to this point. I needed her to know and understand, too.

I moved off the bed, even though I wasn't actually on the bed, into one of the chairs alongside, still holding Cindy's hand making sure to maintain contact. She followed me slowly as I got comfortable. Then I began, "Honey, I want to tell you what happened and how you ended up here, but as I begin I want to ask you to share in the comfort I've found in accepting this whole situation as being directly from God's hand. There are so many puzzle pieces that have come together that only He could have orchestrated and designed to bring us to where we are right now. So as I tell this to you, know I love you more than I can express, but God loves you even more."

I knew the words I had just spoken were almost rhetorical in a way because Cindy's deep love of God and His Word are unshakeable. She has always been so much more mature than I in her view of life and how she handles just about anything. I couldn't have asked for a more solid, stable and strong woman to spend my life with on this earth. From our early marriage to life in the jungle, where life was plain hard, Cindy was unfailing in her strength and support. Now it was time to tell her how she went to the edge of death and eternity, but God decided to have her turn around and come back. I was a little nervous as I began, simply because I didn't want her to be disappointed in me for holding her back.

I began outlining the series of events that took us back to Thursday morning. The memories were still so fresh. Even though I had shared the details with family and several close friends already, looking into Cindy's loving eyes made the telling all the more miraculous.

As I began the account, it quickly became clear Cindy had no recollection of what happened. She neither remembered my kissing her elbow when I came back to bed that fateful morning nor gaining consciousness while being loaded into the ambulance.

"When I heard you hit the floor, I thought at first you had bumped the door on the way to the bathroom, but then I saw you collapsed, lying there off the end of the bed. My next thought was you had a dizzy spell and passed out," I explained as Cindy drank in every word with her limited energy. "Before I was off the end of the bed, I could see you were in full seizure, honey. It wasn't a pretty sight." Recounting the details for Cindy was difficult, also therapeutic, an exercise in healing from the trauma I had been through.

Cindy pressed my hands firmly with assurance as tears flowed freely down my face. "When I made it over to you, I gathered you in my arms, but knew to get you on your side so if and when you came out of the seizure you would be in a good position to breathe and not choke. It was then I had to make a decision." I paused looking into Cindy's big brown eyes. "Honey, I know you aren't afraid to die, but I also knew I couldn't let you go at that time. I had to give you the chance to at least survive this. And while it was, in reality, a short moment in real-time, I made the decision to call 911; it seemed more like a lifetime to make the decision. I didn't want to see you go, and I didn't want to see you held back. I didn't want to be selfish, and I didn't want to be guilty of not trying to save your life. So I decided to call because, if you were to leave me, it wasn't going to be on our bedroom floor; it was going to be on the way to the hospital, or in the hospital or here in Fargo where I knew I had given you the chance to pull through this. I couldn't live with the thought of not trying. Do you know what I mean, honey?"

Cindy's response came with a slow nod as she looked into my eyes. I felt that she understood and accepted the decision I had made. She held me in her eyes with a soft and comforting gaze, the encouragement I needed to continue the story. Her understanding gave me the courage we would both need to continue this journey. I knew in that moment even though her body was weak and in the early stages of recovery, her heart and spirit were fully able and willing to make the journey with me.

I somehow managed to continue through the chronology of the events of Thursday morning, explaining the second seizure in the ambulance, the intubating at the ER in Bemidji and the airlift to Fargo.

"Honey, when you arrived here the situation was dire. It was a race against the clock to get your EVD in place to relieve the mounting pressure in your head and then get inside to repair the aneurysm," I explained in as much detail as I thought she could handle. But at that point, I could see a question came over Cindy about the repair. Neither one of us had ever heard of the coiling procedure nor were we aware of accessing the brain through an angiogram beginning in the femoral artery. "They actually entered through your leg and went all the way up into your head to repair the aneurysm, honey. The procedure went as it should, but after they pulled all the gear out, you had a second hemorrhage, so they had to go back in and repair that one."

I paused to let comprehension dawn. "Honey, if the first aneurysm wasn't bad enough, you had a second one," I said gently, but emphatically. "And yet here I am telling you about it. And you're hearing me. And you're responding to me. And your body is responding to me. I thought I was going to let you go be with Jesus. And you know I was okay with that. And I know you were okay with that. But for some reason, the decision was made that you were to stay, and we have to be okay with that too."

It was time for me to return the enveloping hug of understanding and comfort, so I stood slightly and reached around Cindy pressing my tear-soaked lips to her warm cheek as I made way to her listening ear. "But I negotiated with God Thursday evening," I resumed in a whisper. "I went before his throne in confidence and poured out my heart in intercession for you and said, 'You know dear Father I'm okay for you to take the love of my life to be with you, but if you decide to let her stay, may she come back 100 percent? That is my only ask.' And when I had presented that to God, I turned back to you and began my death song." Cindy knew exactly what I meant. She needed no explanation, having experienced many of those songs in the tribe together with me.

"But God stopped me, honey," I continued after a long intimate pause of just being close to my best friend of three decades. "He didn't want me to sing my song of our lives together because it's not over yet. We get to continue to live it."

I thought back to the time we were home on leave, and I needed to get my wedding band repaired. The ring had cracked, breaking what represented the never-ending love and commitment we had given to each other the day we said our wedding vows. I took the ring into the jewelry store where Cindy had purchased it, Ken K Thompson, and presented it to the gal working the counter, "May I get my wedding band repaired? It has cracked clean across."

"Sure," the pleasant lady said, holding out her hand accepting the transfer of the band from my fingers. She took the ring with care and inspected it momentarily. Before saying anything about the crack, she read the inside of the band to herself, "Love ya forever, Cindy 07-11-87." The gal looked up at me with admiration and said, "Wow, you've been married a long time. That's not too common nowadays."

"Unfortunately, you're right," I concurred with a sad nod of my head. "Our culture doesn't fight for what's worth fighting for anymore. It's too easy to give up and throw in the towel. Marriage is just plain hard work at times, but I can honestly say, when you do the hard yards together, you become the best of friends over time."

"Well, that's the kind of marriage I want someday," the young gal affirmed, dropping the ring in a little plastic ziplock bag. "Do you have a name and number I can put on the bag for when it's ready for pickup?"

That simple little memory came to mind because the gal was amazed we had made it to the 20-year mark of our marriage. And now God had decided we weren't stopping at 33 years.

| day 6
interview

It was interview day. I couldn't believe we'd already been in Fargo for a week. How could the time have gone so fast and yet so slow at the same time? The kids and I discussed heading back to Bemidji, doing the interview with the county and spending the night. My older sister Debbie suggested that even though I didn't want to be away for long, a little break could be good after an intense week of being in ICU.

I got over to the hospital a little before 8:00 a.m. to see Cindy before heading back home. I tried not to burst into the room, but I couldn't help myself. She was still sleeping and looked so peaceful to me. I gently put my hand on her face and whispered, "Good morning, beautiful."

Her eyes opened slowly with a boost from her tired smile. "You're so gracious," she whispered back. "My hair hasn't been washed since who knows when and you still think I'm beautiful?"

"No doubt about it, and besides, any hairdo is better than the Medusa hairdo you had a few days ago," I countered knowing Cindy would have no recollection of the 24 hours of EEG monitoring on day one. "How was your evening?" I continued.

Cindy let out a tired sigh. "Not so comfortable," she stated in fatigued frustration. "The cramping in my thighs has been bad."

"I'm so sorry, honey. I guess it's just gonna take some time to get through that. I'll make sure the kids and whoever is visiting will help massage them for you. We still have the option of stronger meds if you would like."

Cindy pondered the option for a moment and then said slowly, "I'm good sticking with the Tylenol and Ibuprofen for now."

"If you can manage that way, I'm right there with you, honey." I waited a little bit before speaking again. "As soon as the girls show up, I'm heading home for the day, and I'll probably spend the night, too. I have my interview after lunch, so leaving now will also give me time to get ready and do a little yard work while home."

"Sounds like a good plan," Cindy agreed. "I'll have plenty of company while you're gone, but be sure you come back," she quipped with a slight smile.

"Of course, I will. That's not even an option." I said bending over to give her another kiss on the forehead. The door clicked open and Essie and Jordan arrived. I let them take over, and I slipped out to begin the drive back to Bemidji.

The walk through the hall of the ICU to the elevators and down to the parking lot was different this time. Cindy was still not quite out of the woods, but I knew I could leave for the day knowing I'd return to her in recovery mode, even though still critical. I swung the car onto I-94 amidst the busy 8:00 a.m. traffic and flipped on Glenn Beck to accompany me for the ride home. And this time, I actually heard what he was talking about.

The drive was so pleasant compared to the week before. My heart was full of thankfulness to God and what he had brought us through thus far. The timing of every aspect was all God and his sovereignty. I had wanted the interview with the county the day after receiving the email. Now, I was glad the interview was Wednesday. Cindy was stable enough, and my mind was clear enough to think. I like morning interviews, but picked the 2:00 p.m. slot. That gave me enough time to see Cindy, drive the two and one-half hours home and not feel rushed. It also gave me time to decompress, mow the yard and let the chickens out of the coop. Poor free rangers had been confined to their residence for the past seven days. I knew Cindy was in good hands, both with medical personnel and family, so I could relax.

It was a little emotional turning down the lane to our lake home and even more emotional when I pulled into the garage. The house was dark and so quiet. I just stood inside the door not knowing what to do next as memories of the previous Thursday flooded my mind. Cindy had gone away before to visit the kids in California and Florida, and it always shocked me how quiet the house was and how little I talked when she was gone. But now was different. Now the house was heavy with melancholy and memories I didn't care to relive.

> The house was dark and so quiet. I just stood inside the door not knowing what to do next as **memories of the previous Thursday** flooded my mind.

"Dave, pull the curtains open. Let the sunshine in," I told myself. I dropped my backpack, headed for the living room windows and pulled open the curtains to be greeted by the lake. The beautiful sunshine shimmering on the water helped dissipate the trauma I was reliving. I wanted more. I opened the shades in the dining room, at the patio doors and in the master bedroom. Sunshine flowed in, filling me with hope and warming my heart. It reminded me God was still in control of my life and of the natural world, including the sunshine now pouring through the windows into my heart.

My next steps came as naturally as a plant breaking through the soil to greet the nourishing sun. Get some food from the freezer so it thaws out for supper, throw your laundry in the washing machine, get your good suit out of the closet downstairs and make sure it's presentable, find your good shoes to go along with the suit, make sure you have a shower and a splash of cologne. I asked no questions, just snapped to attention, and followed the orders my mind was now barking out like a drill sergeant at marine boot camp. Before I knew it, I was dressed and ready for the interview.

Raised as a military kid, I arrive early for everything, usually 30 minutes early, a bit too early by some estimations. So, I planned to arrive at the county administration building exactly 15 minutes before the scheduled interview, which meant leaving the house about 20 minutes prior. The timing worked well, and I made my way to the second floor HR office and announced I was there for a 2:00 p.m. interview. I was kindly shown a seat and told my interviewer would arrive momentarily.

I wasn't nervous about the interview; I had done them before, and I was confident in who I was and how to present myself. The feeling I had in my gut was similar to every hockey game I ever prepped for—confident, but not overconfident. Sure of my abilities, but ready to adjust on the fly. My plan was not to let anyone know my current circumstances, but to present myself and who I was...prior to the events of the past Thursday.

The wait wasn't long. As I thanked God for the opportunity and reminded Him it'd be a great idea if I got this job, the door from the hall opened, and from behind a masked face a familiar voice greeted, "Dave Wall, how are you?"

"Will, how are you? What a great surprise," I beamed, not letting on that I was a little caught off guard and conscious that I had forgotten my mask. Will was an acquaintance from church whom I hadn't seen in a while, but somehow managed to pull his name out of the recesses of my mind. *Thanks, Lord. That was a huge help to start off the interview on the right foot,* I thought to myself.

"This is great you've accepted our offer to interview here at the county," Will began. "Come with me, and we'll head to the conference room where my coworker is waiting." The two of us headed out the door chatting about not seeing each other for what seemed like forever.

The interview began in a huge conference room that enabled us to social distance properly. We didn't quite need a cell tower between us, but it was close. Will joined his coworker on the other side of the large table, and we began the interview. They worked their way through a prepared set of questions on a sheet of paper for me to follow. Each question was asked clearly. I simply had to give an answer based on my experience from the past outlining how I handled a situation by assessing it, formulating a plan of action and then implementing a strategy to solve it. My only challenge in this type of interview was deciding which of the two million stories I could tell from my years of experience working with people and being in leadership roles. But on the plus side, I love to tell stories, and by the time we reached the last question on the sheet, I felt confident I had presented myself honestly and accurately.

"Dave, we have come to the last question on the list," Will announced with a smile behind his mask. "I know I speak for both of us that your responses to all the questions have been both informative and entertaining, to say the least. But now we want to ask the all-important question of 'Why should we hire Dave Wall?'"

I began my answer, thankful I had forgotten my mask. I wanted the two to see who I was and to see that the expressions on my face matched the passion in my voice. "You know guys, I'm sure the technical side of the position you are offering won't be a challenge for me as I'm pretty good in the whole computer knowledge area, so that's not a concern for me. What I bring to the table and what I hope you have picked up in our time together, is that joining your team will be an addition that will strengthen and move your team forward. I am a team player who is willing to do the hard yards of learning and training from the ground up to become someone you can count on to get the job done. Based on the real-life situations I've shared with you today, that is who I am and what I have to offer."

The interview concluded with an exchange of pleasantries minus any handshakes and before long I was headed back home feeling as if I had presented myself the best I could. But now the waiting game for a phone call began.

My afternoon and evening were busy with yard work, picking veggies from the garden and making supper. I had so much to do that time just flew by. But at bedtime, I just lay on my side of the bed staring at the ceiling. I wasn't restless in the sense of being uncomfortable or overcome with anxiety about the events of the day or what the future might hold; I was just alone.

While I was home, Cindy had continued to struggle with painful cramping in the thighs and of course extreme fatigue. But in the win column, she was able to make it to the bathroom with help from some nurses and a walker. Speech therapists had come to her room and evaluated her speech and ability to swallow, giving the all clear so she could move to a regular diet of food. The neuro team stopped by and decided to turn off her brain drain for several hours to test pressure build up in the skull. The assessment went well even though it'd be a week or so before they removed the EVD for good.

Cindy was also able to venture out of her room for the first time to do some walking in the ICU hall. I wish I had been there, but I know the kids were thrilled to be able to witness that accomplishment. A caravan of gear and hospital personnel accompanied her on her first jaunt around the fifth-floor wing. She had a walker for stability, nurses on the flanks and rear. One nurse managed the brain drain to make sure the flow was not too fast while another nurse managed two IV poles with mobile pumps for the excursion. Thankfully there wasn't a code blue somewhere else on the ward while the entourage made its way through the hall; the traffic jam would have been colossal.

Back in her room, it took nearly as long as her walk to get her settled again and all the bells and whistles back in place. But the effort had been so worth it. Cindy was completely exhausted and instantly fell asleep.

| day 7
danger zone

I left home at the crack of dawn so I could get back to Fargo by 8:00 a.m., the start of visiting hours. As I pulled into the hospital parking lot, I wondered what it would be like to leave with my wife for the first time. The thought of her being released seemed so impossible. Just one week into recovery there were still so many unknowns to be addressed. What would a full recovery look like? What about the vulnerability of stroke? What about memory issues? What about extended therapy? Would Cindy ever be able to watch the grandkids again? I chose to tuck the questions back into the box of my mind and lock it again for another time. The questions couldn't be answered today, and there was no use getting bogged down with trying to figure everything out now.

With the car parked for the day I made my way to the large entrance of the mammoth structure, greeted the valets, went through the screening with the gals at the front and then made my way once again to the 5th floor. I quietly snuck into Cindy's room and stood by her bed putting my hand on her face. "Hey, honey. I'm back," I whispered directly to her.

Cindy slowly opened her eyes timed perfectly with a slight smile, "I missed you while you were gone." Those words never meant more to me. I did a lot of traveling for work in years gone by, and I was always glad to get home to my family. But now, after spending my first night away and alone, the response of missing me was priceless and beyond value.

"I brought you something from home," I continued trying to build a little suspense for the moment even though Cindy's excitability level was challenged.

"Really?" came the tired response. "That was thoughtful of you."

Because Cindy was having such a hard time warming up, Essie was sure to text me at least a hundred times the day before to bring a toque back for Cindy. Now, I should give a lesson on what a toque is for those not from Canada. When it's cold in the dead of winter, you have to cover your head with something to keep warm, and therefore Canadians wear a toque (too-k) on their heads. In the U.S. it's called a beanie, winter hat or even a stocking cap. But for a Canadian, there's only one word—toque. And I had the perfect one for Cindy, my Tim Horton toque. Can't get any more Canadian than that.

Filled with all the excitement of a child giving his parent a gift at Christmas, I pulled the black Tim Horton embroidered toque from my backpack and presented it to Cindy. Her expression lit up the room like the warmth of a hot cup of cocoa on a cold winter's night. "Shall I put it on you," I said.

"Sure," came the soft response with closed eyes waiting in anticipation of feeling warm again.

I carefully pushed Cindy's hair back on both sides of her head and gently pulled the toque down, paying extra attention as I did so keeping an eye on the EVD. Right away, you could see satisfaction come across Cindy's face as the toque trapped in the heat she desperately longed for in her hospital bed. It gave me such satisfaction to see how such a simple gesture could bring so much joy to my dear wife. The only tiny little drawback was that I wasn't holding a cup of Timmy's while enjoying the occasion. I made a mental note: text daughter-in-law for another cup of her amazing brew.

Cindy was able to sneak in a few winks of comfortable rest with her new headgear, but before long it was time for another response test administered by the faithful RN's. "Cindy, how are you today?" the new RN asked with the volume of a yodeler in the Swiss Alps. I now realized the toque was also going to double as hearing protection for Cindy.

Cindy stirred from her short nap and answered, "I'm okay." You could see that she wasn't thrilled to give up her moment of warmth and comfort, but she was sure not to answer in a snarky way.

"I'm going to ask some questions if that's ok?" the nurse continued.

"My name is Cindy Wall. I am 55 years old. I was born April 1, 1965. I'm in the hospital in Fargo. I had an aneurysm, and the month is August. Did I miss anything?"

The nurse turned to me trying to contain her laughter. "Well, I guess that's a full pass on your cognitive response test," she managed with a slight chuckle. "Let's just move on to your legs and arms, shall we." Cindy continued the rest of the exam with little excitement as she wanted to return to the comfort of a little more sleep and the warmth of her toque.

During the day, more visitors arrived, all subject to the "two-at-a-time" rule. Our visitors all waited at the outdoor daycare. Our kids enjoyed meeting so many folks who had a special relationship with their mother. The diversity of visitors was also quite impressive—white folks from northern Minnesota, black folks from the south, Chinese friends, former coworkers from our days in Papua New Guinea and many others. All came just for a short visit with a woman who had touched their lives in some way, and in doing so touched our family with valuable encouragement and strength.

Later in the afternoon, it was my turn to accompany Cindy on a walk around the ICU ward. It was my first time for an excursion of such magnitude, and I vowed I'd never complain again about waiting for my wife to hurry up and get ready. The effort and coordination for such a simple task as a walk around the ward were complex. It reminded me of Operation Overlord in 1944 when the allies landed in Normandy. Cindy's resolve to recover was a match with Eisenhower's determination to take the beaches that fateful day 70 some years ago. She understood clearly that as much as her body wanted to rest, she needed to command it to get up and move. Rest was good, of course, but the need to get the joints and muscles moving was part of reclaiming her health taken by the enemy a week prior. Cindy made it this far, and she was taking back the beaches albeit one step at a time.

> "You know, honey, we're gonna have to work on traveling a little lighter."

When the mobile pumps, IV trees, catheter and brain drain were in position and manned by a nurse on the flank and rear, we headed out the door with Cindy driving the walker and me at the helm. The caravan was sure to let Cindy set the pace.

"You know what, honey," I said as we were a few steps down the hall making sure I didn't walk too fast or slow causing Cindy to bump into me, "We're gonna have to work on traveling a little lighter."

That got a slow eye roll from Cindy as she had us all stop so she could admire one of the paintings hanging on the wall. "I'm really impressed at the choice of artwork here," she began. "Each one is a landscape from around the area, and they are all so pleasant and peaceful." We moved down the hall, and Cindy continued to give her commentary on each piece of art produced by local artists. "I'm going to try to memorize each painting and the order it is in around the hall," she declared. "Do you think that would be a good exercise?"

"Honey, if you accomplished that, your recovery will have surpassed my recovery from the last concussion I had from hockey. And that was 30 years ago."

"You're too funny," she responded with a loving smile.

As we rounded the corner at the end of the ward my mind was in a slow vortex of turmoil. I was thrilled to see Cindy up and moving, but I was also concerned about how much she looked like an old woman as she gripped the walker and shuffled along in her sock feet. One tiny little blood vessel rupture in the command center of the body had sucked every ounce of strength and energy out of her body. The fight to get back was going to take time and determination. I'm not schizophrenic, normally, but I was feeling a split personality of hope and despair shuffling down the hall of my mind and the ICU ward.

Back in bed, the exhaustion was palpable. Cindy collapsed body and mind back into bed. "That's all I have to give this time around," she said deflating like a bouncy house after its air blower was unplugged.

"Honey, we are all amazed you can even get up and walk, let alone make a whole lap around the ward."

"Yeah, I bet I set a speed record this time too," came a sarcastic quip with half a smile as her eyes closed to end the session for another day.

"Every single move you make is a new record," I affirmed with a final kiss to the forehead. And she was asleep.

It was the end of day seven and it looked as if we made it through the vasospasm danger zone. Tomorrow would tell for sure, as the doctor scheduled an angiogram to see how things actually looked in the brain. As I stood over my determined yet exhausted wife, I chuckled to myself, "It wouldn't take long to assess my brain activity."

| day 8
angiogram

During one of my ICU visits, the subject of my beard came up, and Cindy said she'd prefer a goatee. Well, when in ICU you pretty much get whatever you wish for, so I did better than a goat and shaved it all off. Cindy prefers that smooth face of mine anyway, and I'd figured, why not? Anything to make her happy and surprised. If nothing else, it would be some healthy brain stimulation for her to see a change in my appearance. And it might make her chuckle.

When I got to Cindy's room on Day 8, I could see her discomfort, not the way we wanted to start the day. I massaged her thighs and then tried to add some levity to the room and announced excitedly, "Honey, I can't wait any longer. I brought you something."

"What is it?" came the light whisper of a reply from behind closed eyes.

Trying to build some anticipation for the unveiling, I moved closer. "You'll have to open your eyes," I coaxed.

Her battle-tired eyes slowly opened and worked to lock into mine. I slowly pulled down my mask to reveal my clean-shaven babyface. Ok, that's a little strong. Her eyes brightened instantly with approval, "You look so nice!" she declared lifting a hand to touch the fresh surface that had been mossed over since early January. I leaned in a little further, quick to offer a little test run of a smooch, and to my pleasure, she took me up on it.

"Oooo, that's nice and smooth," she announced slowly moving her arm further around me to pull me gently in even closer. "What would make it even better is climbing right into bed with me."

"You're so sneaky," I whispered in return, revealing her mischievous plan. "But I'm still not allowed to get in bed with you."

"But it would make me so much more comfortable," she countered. "It's like it's always moving. Is that just my imagination or is it actually moving up and down?"

I hadn't paid much attention to the bed, but sure enough, as I inspected it, air would fill certain parts, deflate and then rise in another section. It was subtle and hard to notice without actually being in the bed.

"No, you're not imagining anything, honey; the bed is definitely moving," I confirmed. "I wonder if it isn't to prevent bedsores."

"Well, it's definitely to prevent a good sleep," she quipped with a bit of sarcasm.

The analysis of the bed movements disappeared with the ultrasound crew entering the room for yet another round of gel and blue markings. The day had officially begun. The ultrasound would be followed by response tests and a new torture, a needle to the belly to prevent blood clots from forming in her legs. Once again, rest was a rare commodity in ICU, but we were thankful for the amazing care of the Sanford medical team, nonetheless.

Around noon, nurses arrived to prep Cindy for a trip to the OR for her angiogram. While they were getting the bed ready to roll with all her attachments, I met with Dr. S in the hallway to discuss all the potential risks of the angiogram. Even though he was much shorter than I am, his explanation of entering Cindy's body through the femoral artery and traveling up to her brain was way over my head. Upon completion of the dissertation, Dr. S said, "There is a one percent chance of lethality with this procedure; may we have your consent to proceed?"

"Absolutely," I replied without a second thought. And as I signed the consent form, I thanked the doctor again for his amazing care of my dear wife.

With signature in hand, the doctor and his nurse practitioner turned and headed for the OR followed by Cindy's caravan of nurses and gear.

Alone in the room, my mind went into overdrive. Would they discover another aneurysm? Would the coiling procedure pass inspection after a week of healing? What about vasospasms? I decided to lie down on the small couch in the room, and in an instant left behind all my questions and fell asleep.

I awoke to Cindy's caravan rolling her back in post-op. Muffled voices of nurses and aides discussed how to best maneuver Cindy back into bed with all her attachments in place, including her cerebral drain. I sat up and just let the crew do their job while observing Cindy, who was still asleep. I shared in her exhaustion, although hers far outweighed anything I was experiencing.

More than an hour later, Dr. S arrived to give me an update. "Mr. Wall," he began in a patient voice knowing I wouldn't understand much of what he said in medical terms. "The procedure went well and gave us a good look at Cynthia's recovery to date. The coiling we did the day of her admittance is presenting well and is performing the job it is intended for, meaning there hasn't been a presentation of further hemorrhage. We did observe some slight vasospasms, so we went ahead and administered verapamil therapy at 20 ml evenly over 5 minutes. This action seemed to quell the vasospasm appropriately. We didn't see any other evidence of further neurological damage. Overall, we are quite pleased with how the angiogram went and the results it produced."

"That is such good news, doctor. Thank you so much for explaining this to me. I'm thrilled we made it through the vasospasm days without any repercussions," I said with a hopeful smile on my face.

"Yes, we are past the vasospasm danger point for all practical purposes, but now we face the next challenge," the doctor noted as he turned a little more serious.

> *There is an issue with how much drainage is coming off the brain. It seems **pressure continues to build**.*

My smile quickly disappeared, and I found myself turning my head slightly, "What do you mean?"

"There is an issue with how much drainage is coming off the brain. It seems pressure continues to build. The drainage isn't slowing down as much as we'd like to see. We'll keep the EVD in place until midweek," the doctor explained. "But it wouldn't be wise to keep it in place much longer as it is an invasive device with the potential of causing infection."

"What are the options if the drainage doesn't slow down satisfactorily?"

"We would proceed with an internal shunt to facilitate the drainage. Not ideal, but it may be the only option."

"Internal?" I queried with the facial expression to match.

"Yes. The shunt would require further surgery and would run down to the abdomen allowing the disbursement of excess drainage."

The thought made me queasy. "And how long would it have to be in place," I inquired further.

"It would be permanent."

Yikes, I thought to myself. That is not an ideal situation. I'll have to get people praying that the drainage slows down so we can avoid that option altogether. My thoughts went back to my intercession on day zero. "Would it be okay not to have a shunt included in the 100 percent recovery, Lord?"

All in all, it was still a positive day. It was time for me to head out. Leaving the hospital was much easier now that Cindy was through the possibility of vasospasms. The whole shunt issue was a concern, but at least the unknown of potential stroke was fading as we moved along in recovery.

I picked up some Chinese takeout and made it back to where I was staying in time for some playoff hockey, an almost perfect way to end the day. A perfect end of the day would have been sharing the takeout with my dear wife... while I forced her to watch hockey with me.

| day 9
who's the doctor?

The morning began back at Cindy's room where she was sleeping peacefully. I didn't want to disturb her so I sat quietly by the bed until she woke up on her own. I noticed the tall office chair at the computer was somehow missing, so I grabbed the wooden chair in the room as a substitute. Cindy's head was positioned toward the window side of the room, so as quietly as possible I lifted the chair to the other side of the bed. When in place I quietly scooted a little closer to the bedside. The noise of the chair rubbing on the floor sounded similar to a biological noise men make when at home in private (typically). I was now in position to visit with my sweetheart when she rolled her head in my direction at about the speed of a hotdog on a concession roller.

"Was that you?" she queried.

"Whaaaa? Are you serious?" I asked simply pleading for a morsel of credit.

"Well, you do it other places all the time," she affirmed as her head rolled back in the opposite direction.

I couldn't help chuckling to myself, "Obviously cognitive and long-term memory skills suffered no collateral damage through this whole ordeal."

Dr. D stopped by a short time later on his rounds to pay Cindy a visit.

It was good to see the doctor, and I appreciated his taking the time to check in on his patient.

"How are you today, Cynthia," he began with a smile mostly hidden by his mask.

"I'm doing well, doctor," Cindy responded and then without a second of hesitation she continued, "And what is your name?"

The doctor suddenly had a look of shock in his eyes as his head cocked back, "Dr. D" he replied.

"And how old are you?" came the second question without missing a beat.

The shock dissipated as he realized what was happening, "I'm 38 years old as a matter of fact."

"And what's your date of birth?"

The doctor provided the date, unable to contain the smile spilling out from behind his mask.

"And where are you today?"

Sheer delight lit up the doctor's eyes as he answered, "I'm in the ICU unit performing a response test where apparently I'm the patient in recovery because the actual patient is recovering so well that she thinks she's the doctor." We all chuckled. "Cynthia, your progress is beyond all our expectations. It is simply incredible. For what you have gone through, all indications of a quality recovery are headed in an excellent direction. Now, let me resume doing MY job and give my fingers a squeeze as we finish YOUR test."

The doctor finished up his visit with Cindy. As he headed to the door, we had a quick discussion on the drainage issue. "I believe you visited yesterday with Dr. S about the drainage concerns, correct?" he asked me in a quiet voice.

"Yes, we discussed the less than ideal shunt option."

"Well," Dr. D began looking back at Cindy who was already drifting off to sleep, "Her recovery is so good it is my hope we won't need a shunt. Let's give it until Tuesday or Wednesday at the latest to make a final decision. Hopefully, we'll see some solid indicators by that point to let us avoid the option altogether."

"Sounds good to me, but you guys are the experts," I replied, trying not to show my anxiety at having to wait.

And with that, the good doctor was off to his next patient.

Cindy wasn't up to doing a walk until about 3:00 p.m. She was just extra tired it seemed. I wasn't wanting to rush her in any way, but I was a bit let down that she wasn't up to her two walks which seemed to be her new goal. I guess it was a downer for me when I left that evening.

| day 10
struggle

Day 10 had a tough start. It was hard to see my dear wife so weak and uncomfortable from being in bed so much. If you've ever met Cindy, you know she doesn't have a lot of padding to spare and had even less now at the 10-day mark of her recovery. I've got all the padding (well less than before, but still more than Cindy). Back when we lived in the tribe, the people thought I wasn't a good husband because my wife was so thin. Being "fat" was a good sign of health and prosperity, and the man with a heavier wife deserved respect. One time back in the late '90s Cindy contracted hepatitis A and dropped to 105 pounds. Thankfully, we were able to get out for some medical help, and she recovered just fine. Now we were in the same place again, and she could have used some extra padding for her weary body.

Not helping the situation was that Cindy had been losing her appetite the last couple days, so we made certain to have meals sent up to the room three times a day. We couldn't force her to eat, but the consistency, if nothing else, would help get her on an eating schedule.

Maintaining a schedule would also help with another issue that was beginning to show, ICU delirium. Delirium is a normal occurrence for ICU patients as they can lose track of time by virtue of the fact they don't leave their rooms and can't tell what time it is. The nurses were skillful in handling

Cindy's mild delirium by directing her statements and questions away from what she wasn't understanding or comprehending.

I was sitting by the bed thinking Cindy was asleep when all of a sudden, she said, "I want you to get me a fish."

Now Cindy loves fish, but this request came out of nowhere, and immediately I knew what was happening. Thankful for the instructions the nurses gave us about possible delirium, I moved up close to Cindy and responded gently, "Honey, when we get back home, I'll catch you some fish." The answer was sufficient, and she dozed off back to sleep.

We tried to get Cindy up for a walk after breakfast, but the pain in her hips was too much, so we decided not to push it any further and let her rest. It wasn't until mid-afternoon when she managed her first walk of the day.

At one point during the day in all the busyness of the ICU, Cindy downed her horse pills and shortly afterward asked, "That costs $2000 every time?"

I wasn't exactly sure what she was referring to, but I didn't want to make money an issue for her to think about. I knew it was an issue because our health share/non-insurance plan was going to fall far short of paying for what could be three weeks in ICU. I sorted my thoughts out and replied to Cindy's query, "Honey, we are at the Red Sea." Immediately I could see understanding and peace come into her eyes. "The situation we find ourselves in is completely impossible and no different from what the Israelites faced when they fled from Egypt. When they came to the Red Sea, they were trapped with no way of escape. Only God could rescue them and give them a way out. They were in the perfect position to trust God. And we find ourselves in that exact same position. The aneurysm is akin to Pharaoh's armies, the sea is what we are going to pass through with whatever your recovery turns out to be, and you know what the mountains are don't you?"

Cindy responded with a slight nod, and I could see she immediately left the impossibility of our situation in the hands of her loving and competent God.

When we were about to end our visiting time, Cindy had a cute request. "Why don't you just piggyback me around the ward," she began, followed by a tired pause. "When I want to walk, I'll get down and walk." Before I could come up with an answer she concluded, "and you could just drag me back to the room when I was done."

Making sure she didn't see how far back my eyes rolled into my head, I reaffirmed with confidence, "Now honey, you'll be able to walk on your own; besides, if I were to piggyback you down the hall, the hospital staff would know you were having too much fun here." I paused to contain my smile, and concluded, "And if I dragged you back to the room, they'd know for sure I'm a Neanderthal husband."

> Cindy responded with a slight nod and I could see she immediately left the impossibility of our situation in the hands of her loving and competent God.

I believe I left on a bit of an upswing as Cindy's appetite began to improve, primed I think, by a bowl of our daughter-in-law Charissa's homemade soup. Seeing her eat and enjoy it made my heart happy.

day 11
rehab?

The day dawned in Room 546 with definite improvement. Cindy was showing less discomfort overall and increased appetite. After a bite of breakfast we set a new longest-walk record. Cindy wanted to see some new paintings down past the elevators on the ICU level. So we did the extra "mile" and went as far as she felt she could manage. We came upon some paintings she hadn't seen before. She noted how pleasant and appropriate it was to feature paintings of the Fargo area countryside. In my heart, I prayed, *Thank you, Lord, for the little yet big things you grant each day.*

At 11:00 a.m. I felt my phone buzz in my pocket. I dug it out and looked at the caller ID. Beltrami Waste. *That's odd,* I thought. *Why would the county transfer station be calling me?* I stepped out into the hall and swiped to accept it with my curiosity peaked, "Hello?"

"Hello, is this Dave Wall?" the pleasant voice asked on the other end.

"Yes, this is Dave."

"Dave, it's Will calling you back from the county. How are you today?"

My eyes went wide with shock. The county was calling me back about the interview. I couldn't let on that I was out of town and for sure couldn't reveal I was in the ICU ward of a hospital. So I sped down the hall to the waiting area and grabbed a seat, all the while trying to keep my breathing calm and even. "Will, great to hear from you. I'm doing just great," considering the circumstances, which I didn't add.

"That's great to hear, Dave," Will followed without knowing where I was. "If you have a minute I'm just calling with our decision after your interview last week."

"Sure, I've got all the time you need today," I answered, waiting for the drum roll to kick in.

"Perfect," Will said with a tinge of anticipation in his voice. "Well, I'll start out by saying you knocked it out of the park at your interview last week." I nearly choked up. "We would like to offer you the position you interviewed for." I wanted to shout, "Yes," but better judgment kicked in. I didn't want to sound desperate, even though I pretty much was. "I'd like to go through some particulars of the job before you give me your actual 'yeah' or 'nay'."

"Absolutely, please continue."

Will went on to outline the particulars of the job including the hours of work, benefits, and pay scale. It all sounded like a great package that would certainly meet our needs. But Will stopped short of the formal acceptance question and asked, "Now I see you've also been offered an interview with another department in the county, but Dave, I'd like you to join our department and come work with us. I believe you'd be a great fit with our team."

"Well, I appreciate that, Will," I replied feeling flattered. "You know, Will, I believe it's important to throw everything on the table and weigh options out carefully before making a decision. But last week when you showed up to do my interview, I felt something good about seeing you and having a connection to start off."

"I'll admit I had the same connection, Dave, and therefore I'd like you to consider coming and joining my team here at the county," Will affirmed.

"It would be my honor," I replied only wishing I could reach through the phone and shake Will's hand.

"Wonderful," came the reply back from Will. "Would you be able to come in tomorrow to sign papers for a background check and do a drug test?"

"That wouldn't be a problem at all," I agreed as the wheels in my mind kicked into higher gear forming a plan for another trip home.

"I'll talk with the gals at HR and get it setup. How would 11:15 a.m. work?"

Of course, I didn't let anything slip out in response, but that was a perfect time. It would allow me enough time to see Cindy in the morning and then jet back to Bemidji.

"That would work just fine," I responded as if I were just down the street from Will.

"Excellent, Dave. But I have just one more question if that's okay?"

"Of course."

"Would it be okay if I go ahead and cancel that other interview?"

"Go for it, Will," I shot back with confidence. "I look forward to joining your team."

"Dave, thanks so much for being so easy to work with, and let me say again, your interview was a great time. Your stories grabbed our attention as we visited with you last week."

"Well, I have a few million more that I'm sure you'll get to hear as time goes on," I replied while thinking, *He has no idea what's coming his way.*

"Okay, I won't keep you any longer as I'm sure you have a busy day. Any further questions for me?" Will concluded.

"Umm, oh yeah, what do you think would be a start date?" I asked praying it would be the end of the week considering where I was.

"My best guess with the background check and drug test," Will paused while doing a mental calculation. "Let's tentatively look at two weeks from today, August 31st."

"That'd work for me," I concurred without the slightest hint of the cheering voice inside of me yelling, *That will be perfect!*

My new boss and I said a parting goodbye and I took off down the hall like a rocket gone sideways to get back to Cindy's room. I gently burst into the room and announced to my calm and peaceful wife, "Honey, I got the job!"

"That's wonderful!" came the tired yet elated response. "When will you start?"

"That's the amazing thing. The guy said probably not until August 31st, which will be perfect—depending on when we get released from here, of course."

"I hope we aren't here that long," Cindy added with concern.

> *I was soon to learn after a brain injury, people typically need a lot of rehab to help their bodies **recover** and get working properly again.*

I was about to answer with a few words of encouragement when there was a knock at the door and it slowly opened. "Mr. Wall?" a pleasant young lady asked.

"Yes, I am he."

"Hi, I'm Sarah and I'm with extended rehab planning. I was wondering if we could talk down the hall for a moment?"

"Sure," I replied as my thoughts dropped down a few gears to a slower speed. I hadn't even considered rehab, but I was soon to learn after a brain injury, people typically need a lot of rehab to help their bodies recover and get working properly again. I followed the pleasant lady out into the hallway.

"There's a consultation room just around the corner we could use to sit down in if that's okay?"

"No problem. Lead the way," I said.

We entered the small room furnished with comfortable furniture and equally comfortable artwork neatly hung on the walls. Each of us took a seat and the nice lady began, "My name is Sarah, and I don't want to take a lot of your time, but we should start discussing rehab options for Cynthia. She's doing well considering her situation, but in all likelihood, she will need some intensive therapy to ensure the fullest recovery."

"How do you define 'intensive'?" I asked politely.

"Intensive would mean admission to a rehab center 10-14 days after discharge from the hospital," Sarah replied, making the answer as pleasant as possible knowing there was no way to sugarcoat the truth.

"Whoa, so potentially another 14 days after our three weeks in here," I said aloud, realizing the mountains at the Red Sea just grew even taller with impossibility.

"Correct," Sarah concurred. "That is the typical program length for this type of brain trauma."

"And could this rehab take place back in Bemidji where we are from?"

"Unfortunately, Bemidji's fourth-floor rehab department is completely dedicated to COVID-19 treatment and won't be available," Sarah explained apologetically.

"So our option would be…"

"You would need to be here in Fargo for another two weeks at our rehab facility."

I had to mentally take a deep breath, as I didn't want Sarah to see my response of "you've got to be kidding me!" I managed to keep my thoughts in check as I calmed myself and began pleading with God again for a better solution. The puzzle pieces were not fitting so neatly in my big picture once again.

"Ok, I guess we'll just have to see how things will pan out," I somehow managed.

"Well, I know it's hard to think about staying here that much longer," Sarah concluded with an appropriate measure of empathy. "But we do want the best recovery for your wife as possible."

"Yes, I agree, and we'll do whatever it takes to ensure that."

We exchanged a few parting pleasantries, and then I headed back to the room with a plan not to tell Cindy about the discussion I just had. I needed to consult with God about some of those puzzle pieces first.

Closer to supper time I asked Cindy if I could order a meal for her. She looked at me with a puzzled look in her eyes, "What do you mean order?"

"Oh, they have room service here, and actually, here's the menu. You can order from right here," as I placed the neatly laid out menu similar to a fancy restaurant in front of her.

"What am I allowed to order?"

"Whatever your heart desires, honey."

Cindy held the menu, but then looked at me with a sheepish look, "Can you read it to me? I don't think I'm up to reading yet. It takes too much concentration."

I jumped at the chance and began reading through the list of what didn't sound like hospital food at all. Build your own pizza options, tacos, pasta and other cuisine were all laid out and described in mouthwatering detail. After the last item on the menu, I asked Cindy with all the excitement I could muster, "What'll it be, honey? Great options for a hospital, eh?"

"I dunno," came the uncommitted response. "You decide for me."

I hadn't realized yet but was soon to learn decision making for Cindy would prove to be difficult for her in the days to come. I didn't want to draw unnecessary attention to her difficulty, so I said with Italian gusto, "Lessa try da spaghetti an a meatabolla!"

"Sure, that sounds fine," came her satisfied response knowing she didn't have to make the decision.

I grabbed the room phone hanging on the wall behind the bed, called down to the kitchen, giving the room number and Cindy's date of birth, and placing the order for delivery.

Not only did the food on the menu sound good, it arrived at the room at a comparable speed to Jimmy John's—Freaky Fast. And it looked Freaky Fresh. And further, it tasted Freaky Good for hospital food.

Cindy wanted to feed herself, so she masterfully arranged each fork full of food to assure direct placement into her patiently waiting mouth. Sometimes the task needed two or three attempts. But determined and focused, she persevered. She didn't set a speed record by any means. But at least she didn't get the hiccups as her husband often does when he wolfs down a plate of spaghetti like a Saint Bernard—slobber included.

| day 12
brain fluid

I popped in to say goodbye to Cindy before heading back to Bemidji for my HR paperwork and drug test. She was awake when I arrived, and as I approached her bedside for a good morning kiss, she pointed with her finger and said, "Honey, your tag."

Not sure what she was referring to, I looked down my chest, "What? Is my shirt on backwards?" That wouldn't be out of the realm of impossible. One time when the kids were younger, I was in a grumpy mood all day long only to find out my underwear had been on backward since the morning. "Are your undies on the right way?" has long been family code for "why are you having a bad day?"

"Look at your sticky tag. It's upside down," Cindy clarified.

"Reeeeally?" I responded. I can't even dress myself without my wife's help. Here we are only a few days back from death's door, and she has to notice my visitor's tag is upside down.

A nurse was tending to Cindy's drainage system so I sheepishly asked, "May I have some of her brain fluid? It's obviously better than mine." I adjusted the tag and then continued with the morning kiss, thanking my dear wife for her good care of me.

"I'm going to spend two nights back in Bemidji this time, if that's okay with you, honey," I said as I leaned in close. "There should be plenty of visitors to take care of you while I'm gone."

"That's no problem. I'll be okay," she assured me.

"Good, but I better get on the road. I'm supposed to be at the HR office by 11:15 this morning." And with a parting kiss, I left for the day.

The drive home was much easier than the week before. My mind wasn't drifting quite like it was with Cindy in such a critical state when she was fresh off the intubator. There was the issue of the EVD needing to be removed and the possibility of a permanent shunt, but that didn't bother me as I headed down the road. God had done such a miracle to get us to where we were today, that I was confident he would see us through to the end —whatever that might be.

> *I can't even dress myself without my wife's help. Here we are only a few days back from death's door and she has to notice my visitor's tag is upside down.*

I got to the county HR office in good time to sign all the paperwork. I didn't figure I needed to dress up this time, but I did put my mask on as I went into the building. My drug test wasn't scheduled until after lunch, so I headed to the house for a couple hours.

Entering the garage wasn't nearly so heavy and surreal this week, for which I was thankful. I threw some laundry in, got busy making a bit of lunch, let the chickens out of their prison and put together a plan for getting the yard work done. It almost felt normal except for how quiet it was without Cindy.

I buzzed back into town for the drug test and found myself sitting at the occupational medicine office. I was off in space thinking about the many moving parts of the enormous Sanford Medical entity when I was brought back to earth, "David Wall?"

"Yes, that's me," standing up as I responded.

"Please come with me," a pleasant nurse instructed.

I was taken back to a room and given a plastic sample jar with appropriate instructions. I entered the room shown for me to produce my urine sample, and the door closed behind with what sounded like a locking sound. I filled the jar to the mark and placed it on the shelf as per the nurse's instructions, but then I wasn't sure what to do next. Was I supposed to just walk back out into the hall or what? There was an alarm cord I could pull, but I certainly didn't want to give that a yank. So, I decided to knock on the door to see if I was allowed out. The nurse quickly responded, and then I joined her at the end of the hall where we sat and went through a series of questions. Somehow during the questions, the subject of my Cindy came up and I explained my current circumstances. I'm not even sure how long we talked, but the nurse was attentive to all I shared about faith, love and our relationship with God.

| day 13
drain

I knew I made a mistake after I did it. Since being home and having time to cook, I got all fancy and did up some Cajun marinated pork chops on the grill, accented with tasty fried zucchini and peppers from the garden, along with fresh baby red potatoes smothered in butter. So what was my mistake? I sent a picture to Cindy stating I made enough for two. Nothing wrong with that, except that I just showed proof that I could cook. *Might as well spill all the beans,* I thought to myself. I also made two loaves of fresh whole wheat and flax bread!

Being home gave me the chance to get the yard work done, tend the chicks and pick some garden produce. I was busy, but to be honest, my heart was aching for my wife. Today was the day to remove her drain regardless of the outcome. The doctors didn't want to leave it in any longer for fear of infection. By tomorrow they would decide whether an internal shunt would be necessary. Their decision rested on the pressure Cindy would be able to tolerate.

My mother-in-law, Bonnie, herself a nurse, was in the room visiting Cindy at the time it was decided to remove the drain. So, she called me with an update in the early afternoon. I was on the lawn tractor mowing the grass and had my earbuds in listening to music when the call came in. I powered down the mower and tapped my ear without looking at my phone, "Hello, this is Dave."

"Dave, it's Bonnie."

"Oh hey, how's it going?"

"Well, as best as can be expected, I guess. I just wanted to call and give an update about how the day has gone so far," Bonnie announced.

"That'd be great. Go for it; I'm all ears."

"Ok, I'll do my best to give you the details. They did remove the EVD/drain just before lunch today. Of course, they don't do that in the room here, so they took Cindy down to the OR for the removal. They did a cat scan prior to removal and it showed an air pocket in the ventricle which is a definite concern. Not sure if you know, Dave, but there are two other risks associated with an EVD removal that are even more concerning than the air pocket: the possibility of a hemorrhage and infection."

Trying to process removing the EVD in my mind sent me deep into uncomfortable places in my imagination. The device had been in Cindy's head nearly two weeks and the thought of extraction gave me the willies.

"No, can't say I knew the risks, Bonnie. This is new territory for both of us, and besides, I didn't pay much attention in Biology 10 back in high school. But please continue."

Bonnie picked up where she left off, "During the withdrawal, they were hoping to suck the air out, but it sounds like that wasn't successful, so there are a few scenarios that could take place. Best case scenario is the air pocket gets absorbed and disappears, so they have put Cindy on 98 percent oxygen to assist with that. But the best contributing factor will be the shrinking of the ventricles back down to normal size. They are still pretty enlarged from the blood of the initial hemorrhage on day zero."

"Well, that's the scenario we're going to pray for," I interjected.

"Isn't that the truth," Bonnie agreed.

"But please continue with the other options even though I know what's coming," I conceded.

"Right, but I should mention the good news first before I go on," Bonnie said, remembering to add to what she stated previously.

"I'm always ready for good news these days, please continue."

"Well, as I mentioned when an EVD is removed there is a minimal chance of hemorrhage and infection with the procedure."

"Umm, I thought you said good news," I responded, trying to stay positive.

"The good news is that she's cleared of both of those, no issues at all."

"Man, you had me going there for a second," I responded with an exhale of relief.

"Sorry, I should have mentioned that earlier."

"No, problem. Please continue."

"Alright, the second scenario is if her ICP or pressure doesn't subside or at least come down to a manageable level, they might have to put another EVD in place. But I picked up from Dr. D that indications are on the side of not having to do that."

"Well, I'll take that as more good news," I replied while taking a seat on the steps of our deck.

"So, that leaves the third scenario which is the internal shunt to provide continued draining if Cindy's body can't control or handle the amount of pressure she currently has. That option would require another surgery, and it would be permanent, which I'm sure you were already aware of."

"Yeah, Dr. S and I had discussed that option after Cindy's angiogram late last week. At this point it's looking as if that might be the option," I said with a demonstrably falling tone as I sat looking over the lake. "It certainly isn't what I would wish for, but I guess we'll let the doctors make the call."

Bonnie could sense it getting quiet on the other end of the phone. "I'm sorry I don't have better or at least more definitive news for you, Dave, but there is one last thing."

"No need to apologize. I'm just glad you are there with her while I'm taking this little break. So what's the last thing?"

"Cindy will be on complete bed rest until a determination is made about how to proceed."

"Define bed rest," I asked cautiously.

> "Cindy will be on **complete bed rest** until a determination is made about how to proceed."

"Exactly that. She won't even be allowed out of bed to use the bathroom for the next couple of days."

"That'll go over like a lead balloon," I was quick to state.

"Yeah, that's going to be hard for her, having come this far," Bonnie agreed. "Well, I better get back to the room now. Lloyd's still in there with her."

"Thanks for calling Bonnie. I sure appreciate your doing so."

"Oh, absolutely. My pleasure," Bonnie concluded, ending the call.

I sat there with my elbow on my knee and my head supported in the palm of my hand thinking through what was just discussed, wishing we were done with the unknowns. Cindy had survived the initial hemorrhage, was able to breathe on her own after coming off life support, came through the vasospasm forest without a stroke, and has seemingly retained all her cognitive and neurological abilities. But now there was an air pocket in her head? Was I being too selfish to wish or mildly ask for one more hurdle to be cleared? Should I be satisfied with how far we have come and just call it good?

Two grey squirrels grabbed my attention as they chased each other in circles around the trunk of the large basswood tree next to the bird feeder at the edge of the yard. I couldn't help thinking how much they represented my thoughts at the moment as they went round and round. They'd stop only for a second to let their tails twitch up and down, and then resume the chase. They never seemed to catch up to one another, ever. But I didn't want my thoughts going endlessly in circles. I wanted them to slow down, come to a standstill and rest. The problem was what to rest on. Was I okay with less than 100 percent recovery? No, but I didn't want to be demanding of God either. My thoughts went back to day zero and standing before Him alongside Cindy in those critical early hours. I asked for 100 percent at that time without a thought of being selfish or demanding. Sure, I was ready to accept the other 100 percent and let her go, but I asked for 100 percent either way. Why wouldn't I continue to do so? And that's when the chasing subsided. Contentment came with settling for a 100 percent answer to my initial request. I wasn't sure how we'd get there, but it wasn't my job to figure that out. My job was to simply keep trusting.

I unpaused Pandora, hopped back on the tractor and finished mowing nice straight lines now that my mind wasn't going in circles. Unlike the crazy pair of squirrels, still chasing each other around the tree trunk.

| day 14
hurdles

I could have driven back to Fargo with my eyes closed that morning. But, of course, I didn't. Dawn is time to be on full alert for deer in northern Minnesota. It's not uncommon to see a fresh deer carcass on the roadside on my morning drive to town. It's so bad that come fall, one of the auto body shops has a contest for the worst deer hit, offering a hundred dollar gift certificate for the repair. Only in northern Minnesota.

Part of the way to Fargo, I stopped at the Park Rapids McD's for a couple of breakfast burritos and a coffee refill. I had to leave home so early to make visiting hours that I skipped making breakfast at home. Cindy would be so surprised hearing I actually went to McD's as I normally avoided the fast-food chain like the plague. Oh well, desperate times call for desperate measures. But actually, the burritos aren't half bad… on the road… and when you're really hungry.

Once again arriving at the hospital I had thoughts of when we might get to leave. It was still such a total unknown. Cindy was still in ICU, and the doctors had given no indication of a timeline for discharge. Each time we saw progress, we faced another hurdle. But we had to look forward to the next hurdle, trusting to get over it. When our daughter Maea ran track for NDSU, she was a heptathlete, which included hurdles in her repertoire of events. The concentration that goes into running those things is crazy, not to mention the scraped shins and mistimings that were all too painful. To win the race you had to clear each hurdle before getting to the final stretch where you could pour it on for the sprint to the end. I felt as if we were still clearing hurdles as I entered the all too familiar entrance to the hospital. The sprint wasn't even in view yet, and who knew if we'd have the push to make it to the finish line.

Cindy was looking good as I entered her room, but I could sense a measure of frustration because she was confined to bed rest. "Hey, I'm back," I said, greeting Cindy with a light kiss and hug. "How are you doing?"

"Well, as good as can be expected," came her reply. "I'm not allowed out of bed, and I can't decide if I like the oxygen mask for style or the tube thing in my nose. Neither one goes well with my sore hips from this crazy bed that keeps breathing beneath me."

"I'm so sorry honey," I tried to empathize. "But they have to keep you on bed rest because it appears there's an air pocket where the drain was inserted. The best way to help dissipate it is with lots of straight oxygen and rest."

"I know," came the tired agreement. "But I just want to walk around, because it helps so much with the discomfort."

"I understand, honey, but we have to trust what the doctors are telling us."

"Can you at least crawl into bed with me? I know that'll help," she lightly pleaded.

"No, not yet," I replied as apologetically as possible.

Just then the PA showed up at the room. She was a pleasant gal who, if I had to guess, was nearing her thirties. "How are we doing today, Cynthia?" she asked as she came to the bedside with her hands neatly tucked into the pockets of her white lab coat.

"Ok," Cindy replied. "But I'd sure like to get out of this bed and go for a long walk."

"I bet you would, but unfortunately you're going to have to stay put for a while longer. We have to see some progress with that air pocket and the size of your ventricles first."

I bit my tongue fighting back any airhead comments as I continued listening to the pleasant PA.

"At this point, we haven't seen any change, so I'm going to keep you in bed another 24 hours."

The declaration wasn't what Cindy wanted to hear, but she conceded as she didn't have the energy to argue her case.

"Mr. Wall, would you like to see her latest scan? I can walk you through what we're seeing since taking the EVD out yesterday."

> *Unfortunately, the air pocket in Cindy's brain hasn't gone down much and there is still a **substantial** amount of fluid in the ventricles.*

"Sure, I'd appreciate that," I responded knowing what I would be looking at and what she would be explaining might not line up as they should. Nonetheless, it would help me working with Cindy when it came to keeping her in bed AND keeping me out of her bed of course.

The PA and I went over to the computer station in the room where she logged into the system to pull up Cindy's CT scans. Once the images loaded, the PA took out her pen and pointed to the air pocket that "clearly" showed where the EVD had been placed a full 14 days earlier.

"Unfortunately, the air pocket in Cindy's brain hasn't gone down much, and there is still a substantial amount of fluid in the ventricles," the PA explained as clearly as she could.

My immediate reaction came with semi-squinting eyes while trying to figure out how she got that assessment from the image. "The air pocket looks fairly small," I began. "Pretty sure the one in my head is a large black hole that sucks in massive amounts of empty space the Hubble space telescope couldn't calculate."

A professional and measured giggle came in response. "Well, there is some good news as we keep our assessments current for Cindy's situation."

"What's that?" I said with a spike in excitement. I wanted anything moving in the direction of good news.

"Well, there hasn't been an increase in the size of the ventricles, and that means we are pretty certain the EVD will not need to be reinserted."

"That is good news," I quickly agreed.

"So that means we are still assessing the shunt option because of the size of the ventricles at this point."

"I understand. It's one hurdle at a time isn't it?"

"Very much so. That's a good way of looking at it," she agreed. "So, here's what we'll do. I'll consult with Dr. K, the neurosurgeon who does the shunt placements, and suggest we keep Cindy in bed another 24 hours with the full oxygen in hopes of seeing both the air pocket dissipate and the ventricles contract. Then tomorrow morning we'll order another CT scan and make the call about the shunt, depending on what we see."

I took a deep breath and slowly exhaled as I looked over at Cindy, who had fallen back into some much needed sleep. "Ok, let's keep going."

The pleasant PA left us, and I was alone again in the room that had become all too familiar. I came to the realization in my sea of thoughts that today marked two weeks being in ICU. *Two weeks,* I thought to myself. *How can that be? The days have flown by, but at the same time they seem so long and drawn out, as if they are being played out in slow motion.*

I stood looking over Cindy, once again knowing when she woke, she'd be frustrated to know she was still confined to her bed with tight restrictions. I rehearsed my lines to make the news as palatable as possible, knowing well she wasn't going to be happy no matter how I said it. Losing the opportunity to walk, to take herself to the bathroom and even use the bathroom were going to be hard to take. It felt as if she were going backward, losing momentum. But if we wanted to avoid a permanent implant, we had to follow the advice and direction of the doctors.

| day 15
bed rest

As with each arrival at Room 546, I tried to make the start of the day as cheery as possible. But with bed rest, it became harder to make things bright and positive. Life gets mundane, boring and flat. Something as normal as answering nature's call becomes a luxury. There's no dignity when you are confined to the bed. So how does a guy turn that into a positive? Well, I'm not too sure I figured that one out.

Cindy had to go two times in a row, so I asked as politely as I could muster, "You need to go again?" Remember, I asked politely, but not politely enough. And as the question left my mouth without any chance of retraction, I realized I shouldn't have opened my mouth in the first place. There's sticking your foot in your mouth, but this was akin to sticking your whole leg in your mouth, and my attempt to make the room cheery and bright came crashing to the ground in flames like a Russian missile test.

Her answer came back as smooth as a poker player laying her winning hand on the table in confident victory, "Yes, you inspire me that way." The answer wiped all the chips off the table as it was a direct reference to my pea-sized bladder she has endured and put up with our 33 years of marriage.

There was no comeback. I sat mum, amazed at the wit generated on day 15 in ICU. Her ability to dish out and feed her husband a plate of crow was a miracle in itself. What a victory. What an accomplishment. It was worth 10 laps around the ICU. And I was happy to let her have them all in exchange for enjoying a few moments in her captivity of bed rest.

My full expectation of the day was hearing the dreaded determination Cindy would need a shunt. If that's what was needed to manage the drainage and pressure then I guess I'd have to just buck up and be content with it. Finally, about mid-morning, she was taken for another CT scan. Upon return, she continued to beg to get out of bed, even just to use the bathroom normally.

Around noon, an average height man with a slight build came into the room. I assumed he was a nurse being dressed in scrubs, but I noticed he didn't have an ID badge attached to the pocket, as all the RN's had. He came over to the side of the bed and began to ask some questions, and immediately I picked up on his slight Russian accent. What struck me funny were the questions he asked. It was as if he came off the street and knew nothing of Cindy's two-week stay in ICU or her recovery journey thus far. I actually began to wonder if he was an imposter of some sort. The Russian accent didn't help as I tried to convince myself otherwise. Maybe I was developing ICU delirium.

After the series of questions were complete to his satisfaction, the man began a response test with Cindy, and it finally dawned on me he must be a doctor. So I asked politely, "And who are you?"

"I'm Dr. K," came the response ending in "ov," confirming he was Russian. "I'll be assessing the need to implant a shunt for the patient."

"Oh, so you're a neurosurgeon as well," I responded, giving myself a slap to the back of the head while thinking, *Way to spill the bowl full of suspicious beans all over the place.*

"The air pocket is dissipating well, and the ventricles are looking better than yesterday. I'm going to consult the other surgeons because I don't think she needs a shunt." He wasn't much for conversation, to be honest, but hearing those words was all the one-sided conversation I needed.

The doctor left as quickly as he came in, and as he did so, I hoped he, upon leaving the room, didn't notice my catatonic state.

I was shocked. *No shunt?* I thought to myself, *that'd be too good to be true.* But I guarded my excitement with caution, not wanting to get carried away in premature hope and have to drag myself back to reality like a hot air balloon gone flat.

> *The neurology team concurs; we'll **hold off** on the shunt.*

So far my experience with waiting for results or consultations in the hospital was long and drawn out. I'm sure that was partly because I just sat there waiting instead of going on a road trip or vacation to kill the time. But the doctor turned out to be a functioning Russian rocket and returned way sooner than I expected.

He came back into the room and announced, "The neurology team concurs, we'll hold off on the shunt as progress is heading in the direction of not needing one. Cindy is off bed rest and is free to move about the cabin." Well, he didn't exactly use that metaphor, but the relief Cindy felt was like popping off her seat belt after a longer than usual round of turbulence five miles up. No sooner did the doctor leave, and we had Cindy up for a long walk using up every drop of energy she could muster. Then it was back in bed to rest and recharge so she could enjoy another excursion later.

During Cindy's rest, our son Chas's mother-in-law, Lisa, showed up for a visit, and I relayed the great news about not needing a shunt. In her typical bubbly personality, she responded, "Dave, I just know God is going to completely heal this girl. I just know it! Complete restoration is what we've been asking for, and God is going to grant it." Lisa's faith and trust were such a breath of fresh air. Yes, I was hopeful, but there's nothing like someone showing up who can help charge your exhausted batteries, and that's exactly what Lisa did for me at that point.

Lisa and I visited for a while being sure not to wake Cindy, but before long she was awake and ready to get out of bed again. This time she declared, "I don't want to leave the room. Let's just do some exercise right here in the open area," she instructed the aide to hook the oxygen hose to the portable tank and meet her on the other side of the bed.

I quickly snapped to attention and met her at the bedside to assist her, as I didn't want her to get out of bed too quickly even though it was all in slow motion anyway.

"You think I can't get out of bed by myself?" Cindy quipped as I held her arm to assist. "I know I'm a grandma, and I know I look like an old grandma, but if I'm allowed to get out of bed, I'm getting out of bed."

"That's no problem," I agreed. "But I'm going to help you just the same. I don't want any geriatric moves sending you to the floor."

Pretty much ignoring my concerns, Cindy waved to Lisa and the CNA to join her in the exercise, "Come on ladies, you better join me as Dave won't dance with me."

The ladies started what resembled line dancing in slow motion around the room. I knew Cindy would kill me, but I didn't care about dying at this point, so I whipped out my phone and began taking video of the trio with particular focus on the gal in the middle ornately dressed in an oversized hospital gown along with a matching Tim Horton toque and oxygen bottle in tow. The Liberian CNA was all smiles to see her patient bust out a few moves while holding her hips from the rear just in case she decided to hurl herself to the dance floor—involuntary of course.

It was so good to have the room filled with laughter and enjoy Cindy's comical antics while trying to use every unused muscle in her body after being confined to her bed the past 48 hours. When the last of her energy was spent, I made her get back in bed and eat a bit of lunch. She knew she needed to rest again, but the rest was welcome because she knew she'd be out of bed again quicker than a sea turtle can lay its eggs on a beach and get back into the ocean... well maybe not that quick yet.

It was a good day. I sent the dancing queen video to the kids but didn't post it on social media for fear of ending up in ICU myself.

| day 16
recovery

The day began on a much lighter note knowing Cindy wouldn't need a shunt. I found myself wondering if we'd hit the home stretch of our time in the hospital, but I stopped myself from running ahead. We still had a decision about rehab. Cindy's little jig the afternoon before wasn't quite enough to dismiss the notion of checking in for another two weeks of care in the physio department of the medical facility. Nonetheless, yesterday's progress filled me with more hope than I had experienced for over two weeks.

I hit the McD's on my way to the hospital realizing I'd become somewhat fond of their breakfast burritos and now their Egg McMuffins. I'd mentioned to Cindy I'd grab her one on my way over when I left last evening.

I arrived at "Chatty Cathy's," oops, Cindy's room to find her sitting bedside and in conversation with the nurse's aid while working her way through a breakfast of sausage and gravy over biscuits. Cindy didn't see me come in as she was facing the window side of the room soaking in the sunshine that burned off Fargo's morning fog.

As I came to her side, I could see Cindy was trying to get her Liberian CNA to share breakfast with her. It wasn't the first time she'd tried to share her food, as both she and I knew all the Liberians came from tribal backgrounds similar to what we experienced in Papua New Guinea. In tribal culture, you never eat in front of someone without sharing; it's how they survived. We had to teach our kids if they went outside with a treat, they had to break it into pieces making sure each one of their friends was served a piece. Whether it was a beef cracker (large, seasoned crackers) or a bag of Twisties (similar to Cheetos that the people call shrimp brains), the kids learned to share equally with their friends. We felt it was important we assimilate to the culture in appropriate ways, and sharing food when outside was one of those ways we drilled into our kids. So here was Cindy, trying to get her aide to eat with her, but the aide politely refused knowing it was against policy to do so.

Cindy saw a bag in my hand as I came closer and realized she forgot I was taking care of breakfast. "I'm sorry, honey. I forgot you were bringing breakfast," she managed to confess through the delight of her biscuit-filled mouth.

"It's okay, honey. I got up extra early to get on the journey over here, but I'm good," I falsely confessed, rubbing it in for a bit of false guilt effect.

Cindy turned to the aide, her apparent ally, and declared in a lower tone, "He never goes to McDonald's." The "M" on the bag ratted me out.

"But I did wait a long time in the drive-through!" I added to gird up my crumbling defense.

Didn't work, but Cindy was gracious enough to eat half a bacon egg and cheese McBiscuit thingy while continuing to coax the aide into sharing with her.

I pulled up a chair, making sure it made no embarrassing noises, and joined the two ladies in their conversation. The room was oddly quiet. Normally the hospital staff would be stopping by in timed succession checking on Cindy, but no one was showing up, not even the ultrasound crew to reink the temples of Cindy's head.

The aide informed me another CT scan had been done early in the morning, and we should be expecting an update at any time. I still refrained from any airhead jokes, and in my heart, I was desperately hoping we could continue to progress from yesterday's great news of foregoing the shunt option.

Both Cindy and I finished up our somewhat enjoyable fast food breakfast and began to prep for a walk around the ward.

"Hey, we're down to only one attachment," I declared. "Just an oxygen bottle to tow along."

"Well, two actually," Cindy corrected sheepishly. "I still need the walker if we're going to leave the room."

"I guess that's true, but only one is attached to you. So that's a plus," I reaffirmed positively.

The aide worked at attaching the airline to the oxygen bottle making sure the pressure was set properly, and I unfolded the walker and put it in position on the door side of the bed ready for Cindy to spring into action. Well, it wasn't quite a spring yet, but she had moved on from sea turtle speed.

Just as Cindy was about to swing her legs to the side of the bed, her PA arrived at the door with a spring in her step. "Santa Claus is here," she announced with a spark in her eyes. "Cindy, your CT scan shows a decrease again in the air pocket and, even better, a significant decrease in the size of the ventricles."

"Praise God!" I blurted out before the PA could continue.

"We are therefore going to release you from ICU—today."

I couldn't believe what I just heard. Never in my entire life was anything said so beautifully as that. Of course, the exchange of our marriage vows was beautiful, but decades later when my best friend had been given a new release on life, the words were so much more beautiful.

"Cindy, I want you to know you are a complete miracle," the PA continued. "Two weeks ago, when you arrived by airlift, your head was so full of blood we wondered how you would survive. And now I'm putting in the order to move you out of ICU with a fully-functioning recovery."

"People all over the world have been praying," I interjected, affirming the miracle.

"I can SEE that," the PA concurred in all sincerity.

Glory be to God! When Cindy was extubated 48 hours after her initial aneurysm it was inexplicably similar to a newborn baby's first breath—life had begun. She gasped, squirmed and with the life that only the Creator can give becoming a living person—again. Yes, what a miracle we have witnessed. Cindy was born as an infant—a miracle, born again as a child of God—a miracle, and now a third time has been "born again" to continue living for her Savior—a miracle. We had witnessed a truly win-win situation. If Cindy had not survived that first trauma, she would have won by gaining heaven. We were prepared for that as a family, but now that Cindy was going to pull through this whole ordeal, we also had a win because she would continue to live for Christ.

The PA continued, "I'll put the orders in to get a room ready in the neuro-recovery wing."

"So you mean we could leave the ICU today?" I asked, still in shock from what I was hearing.

"If there's a room open, then hopefully this afternoon, or at the latest tomorrow morning, we can transfer her over there."

I turned and looked at Cindy with wonder in my eyes. "Honey, can you believe that?"

"That means if you get me out of this bed, I could get two walks in: one last walk around the ICU ward and then a walk over to recovery," Cindy replied half joking to remind me of the intention to get moving and out of bed.

I turned back to the PA as I moved in position to get Cindy started on her walk, "Thank you so much. I think I'm still in complete shock and unbelief. I'm sure you've seen your share of patients who don't get this kind of news."

"Yes, that is true. While we work hard to see every patient recover fully, it isn't always the case. But today is not one of those days," the PA responded with glee. "So, I'm going to leave you to your walk and get those orders in right away."

"Thank you again," I said as I repositioned the walker for Cindy. "Now let's get you ready to tear up the halls of the ICU one last time, young lady."

"Ha!" Cindy responded as she slid off the bed into her flip flops waiting below. "I don't know about the tearing up or the young, but I'm thankful I can walk nonetheless."

Just as we were about to begin our excursion Maea arrived and joined our little entourage heading down the hall. I shared the great news of getting the all clear to leave the ICU, making a mental note to text the other kids right after the walk.

The excursion around the ward felt so different. Kind of the feeling you have when you've taken your last exam at the end of the school year. You walk back to your locker feeling the relief of being done. Yet because you've spent the last ten months in the same mode, you're not quite ready to believe you're truly done. You're smiling big on the inside and outside, but until you clean out your locker and actually leave the building, you're not quite ready to explode with excitement and relief.

We came to the windows at the end of the hall, and I reminded Cindy that right below was the outdoor "daycare" where our family had spent so many days. Cindy paused and looked out the window enjoying the bright sunshine of the day and the endless view of the city that was once flat farmland for as far as the eye could see.

"I'm so thankful for such a supportive family," she said looking off in the distance, with Maea at her side resting her head on her mom's shoulder.

I tried not to choke up at the comment and didn't reply because I knew I wouldn't even be able to talk after a statement like that.

But then Cindy turned to me and dammed up any potential tears by saying, "We should dance."

My jaw dropped open. I looked at Maea with squinting eyes and pointed to her mother, "You know I've been noticing your mother has somehow developed a real sense of humor through this whole ordeal. Something happened upstairs, and she's actually become funny. It's like a log jam of humor has loosened and is now flowing freely down the river of her mind to her tongue."

"Come on, dance with me, honey," Cindy continued to nag.

"I still can't dance. Let's keep moving. I wouldn't want someone to think I was the one recovering from brain trauma," I answered, stiffening my frame in resistance.

We continued our trip down the corridor sans any dance moves and made it back to the room. A young male nurse named Joey was at the computer entering updates. "Hey, I heard the good news. You get to move to recovery, and it looks like a room is ready. Up one floor to number 612," he exclaimed in an excited voice.

"You mean you want to get rid of me?" Cindy countered with a joking smile.

"We love getting rid of people—in the right way of course," Joey was quick to clarify. "Especially when they start out the way you did and make a recovery like you have. I attended you on your first night, and to be completely honest with you, we didn't think you were going to make it." We all turned a little serious for a moment and then the nurse continued, "Your recovery has been nothing short of incredible, and I am thrilled to see you moving on."

"Well then, I guess you better help us get packed up for the big move. Do you have any boxes?" Cindy asked, already in packing mode as she parked her walker alongside the bed.

"Honey, you just climb back up into bed and let us take care of the packing," I said, jumping into the conversation.

"I'll run down the hall and see what I can find, but I agree with your hubby, back into bed and let us take care of the moving."

"And I'll find a wheelchair for transport," a West African accent closely followed.

I began delicately pulling the myriad of pictures and kiddie artwork off the walls and window, each one a precious gesture of love for their mother and grandmother. Cindy wanted to touch each of them as we waited for a box big enough to hold them all.

Before long, our Liberian CNA returned with a wheelchair and two large boxes for packing up Cindy's treasures. We loaded up the boxes, had a couple of extra-large bags of clothing to add in the mix, a couple of backpacks and, of course, the oxygen bottle. Our CNA was Johnny On the Spot and found a cart to load everything on, and then we began our trip to 6th floor neuro-recovery.

There wasn't a formally organized parade route leaving room 546, but the hall somehow magically lined with nurses, CNA's and hospital workers to wish us well on Cindy's road to recovery. It felt so special knowing all the care that had been extended to us the past 17 days, but the thrill of no longer needing the ICU far surpassed anything as we left our "locker" behind and graduated to a whole new life through the elevator doors we'd become all too familiar with.

As we arrived at 6th floor recovery, I found it funny that recovery was up a floor instead of down, like toward the exit. At least that's the direction I thought we should be heading eventually—out the door on ground level. But it didn't matter as a few short steps out of the elevator we were greeted by the peaceful and enveloping ambiance of the recovery ward. The lack of ICU noise and hustle and bustle was a welcome reprieve. Everything was so peaceful. No one was in the halls. The nurses' station was quiet with just a couple of gals making notes at computer stations.

The CNA gently pushed open the door to the room and wheeled Cindy in. Half a step into the room, I knew I wanted to lie down and rest; it was so quiet and peaceful.

"Do you feel and hear that, honey?" I asked Cindy as she positioned herself to sit on the bed.

"You mean the peaceful feeling. The lack of noise. The fact that no one is rushing into the room."

"Yeah, let's just enjoy it forever," I joked.

Our CNA didn't stay long as I guess she figured she wasn't needed in the recovery wing, but before leaving she got Cindy set up and comfortable in her new bed. Before long we were left alone.

Cindy looked tired from the journey, and as she began to doze off she asked, "Now that we've left ICU, will you finally crawl into bed with me?" Her smile communicated clearly. I no longer had an excuse to deny her request.

"Well, now that we are on a less stressful ward and part way out of the woods, I guess I could go halfway and sit on the edge of the bed."

Cindy wanted a 100 percent but settled for the 50 I offered. I moved my chair to the side making sure it didn't make any offensive noises and proceeded to sit on the bed, confident my negotiation was satisfactory... at least for the time being. I moved in, sat down but instantly shot up like a geyser in Yellowstone National Park. Alarms started ringing and beeping. Nurses and aides came running so fast I was sure they'd been hiding in the closet.

> *Alarms started ringing and beeping. Nurses and aides came running so fast I was sure they'd been hiding the closet.*

"What did I do?" I asked in a state of panic, standing back from the bed. "Is the bed alarmed so I don't get in?" I blurted out revealing my intentions.

"No, no," the RN assured me. "Because Cindy doesn't have a full-time nurse assistant, we had alarmed the bed in case she tried to get out."

"Ohhhh," I said aloud, making sure not to make eye contact with the "prisoner." "I'll just sit over here instead, now that I'm freaked out like a cat on a hot tin roof."

"No problem, I'll just turn off all the alarms as I'm sure Cynthia doesn't need them anyway," the nurse continued as she began pushing buttons to disengage the startling prisoner escape device. "Now, Cynthia, if you need to use the restroom, make sure you push this button right here so one of us can come help you. Just being out of ICU, we still want to provide that assistance for you."

Cindy slowly nodded her head, as she was already headed down the path of a restful sleep, seemingly unaffected by the alarms her husband with the cat-like senses just set off.

| day 17
peaceful

Day 17 arrived and I was still the hustle and bustle mode of the ICU. So, when I knocked lightly on Cindy's door on the sixth floor, I was pleasantly surprised by the peace and calm. Shades on the window gently guarded my sleeping beauty. It was quiet and restful. I so wanted to plant the awakening kiss to start the day, but I could only kneel by Cindy's bed and thank God for allowing me to continue my journey with the incredible woman he had given me.

The moment made me think of Adam when first presented with bone of his bones and flesh of his flesh. His first words were, "Whoa man!" The actual etymology of the word "woman" as he called her. Yeah, the Lord did good meeting Adam's need in the beginning, and he had done the same for me. My heart and soul were gently flooded with the memories of our 33 years together and all God had allowed us to do and experience as a couple. I thought of our five amazing children, our 11 grandchildren, thankful again that Cindy would be able to enjoy them all for another extended period of time. Only God could have made it possible.

Deep in thought, I barely heard the door open as our youngest, Maea, slipped in, respectful of the quiet of the recovery ward. She wanted to see her mom before heading to church.

"Wow, it's so peaceful up here in recovery," she whispered.

"Isn't it amazing," I replied as I stood and gave her a hug. "What did you bring?" I asked, noticing the restaurant take out container she held out to the side making sure it didn't get squeezed between us.

"I figured I'd make some over-easy eggs and fried potatoes for mom. Home cooked of course."

"They let you in with outside food?" I asked a little shocked, forgetting we did bring in Chick-fil-A and homemade soup when in the ICU.

"Nobody asked, so I didn't say anything," Maea responded with a mischievous smile as she gently rubbed sleeping beauty's arm. "Hey, Mom. Are you ready for some breakfast? I brought you your favorite, over-easy eggs and potatoes."

Cindy moved a little making it obvious she had to climb out of the deep and restful sleep she had been enjoying—exactly what recovery was meant for. Her eyes finally opened, "Hey, Maea." She said in a slow, satisfied manner. "How long have you been here?"

"I just got here, and I brought you some homemade breakfast— over-easy eggs and potatoes."

"That sounds wonderful."

"Maybe we can figure out how to tilt the bed up so you can be in a better position to eat," Maea asserted as she began looking over the panel on the side of the bed that was similar to the cockpit of the space shuttle.

"Not so quick there, Maea," I interjected. "Maybe we should push the nurse button as we wouldn't want to set off an alarm or anything."

"Yeah, not like your dad," Cindy chimed in with delight.

"Here you just push this button right here," Maea pointed to and then pushed before I could intervene. "Why what happened?" She said with the look of an expert as the bed lifted Cindy into a sitting position.

"Ahh, it was nothing," I fibbed having had enough embarrassment from the day before.

"Come on, honey. It's a cute story. Tell Maea what happened."

"Okaaaaay," I said slowly, much to the thrill of my wife, as she slowly sampled her over-easy eggs and potatoes.

Maea jetted off to church after her morning mission was complete, and Cindy decided she'd like to do her first walk of the day. "I'm pretty sure the bed is no longer alarmed, honey, so how about we get out of here for a walk?"

"Great idea, let's go explore our new territory," I agreed. "I'll grab the walker for you."

"Actually, I'd like to go without it," she stated, stopping me in my tracks. "I think I can do it just holding your arm."

"Ok, then, just the arm it is. But I better call the nurse to hook up the oxygen bottle as we still need to take that along."

"I suppose," Cindy agreed. "I also want to get covered a little better too. I feel like the back door is wide open in the scanty gowns I've been wearing."

"I know there are some supplies over in the closet; maybe they have another one you could wear backward." I checked around in the closet keeping an eye out for alarm-looking devices and found another gown for Cindy. By the time we got her all fixed up with the second gown, a fleece jacket and her wonderful toque, the nurse had arrived to hook up the oxygen bottle for our excursion.

And before long the two of us were headed down the corridor with one less implement on the road to recovery.

As we slowly walked down the ward, we couldn't get over the peacefulness of the recovery wing. Beautiful artwork hung on the walls between rooms.

All so quiet in the morning stillness. If you happened to pass someone in the hall, you exchanged a friendly nod and said hello.

Cindy felt strong enough to extend her walk all the way over to the cardio-recovery wing as well, fully doubling the length of any previous walk to date.

"We better head back to the room, I guess," Cindy finally said. "Wouldn't want to overdo it you know."

"Hey, it's totally up to you," I encouraged. "You're in charge of the energy meter, so when you've had enough, you've had enough. And there's no reason to rush as we have lots of time to recover." As I spoke, I thanked God again that I didn't have to be back to work until August 31st, giving us plenty of time to see how things would work out with a rehab plan or whatever the doctors decided on for a course of recovery.

On our way back to the room, Chas suddenly came up behind us. "Hey, it's so good to see you out for a walk and without a walker no less," he observed while giving his mom a tender yet all enveloping hug.

"Good to see you, son. Are you by yourself? No littles?" Cindy asked.

"No, I thought I'd buzz down quickly by myself. But I did bring you something I think you'll like. It's already in the room," he said with a big smile showing his missing tooth compliments of a hockey puck last winter.

"Oh? What's that?" Cindy asked.

"You'll have to wait and see, but you won't be disappointed."

"Well then let's just run the last stretch back to the room," Cindy joked with a smile and slow-motion arms movements that indicated she was already moving as fast as she could go.

Back in the room, Cindy found Chas' surprise, the softest and most comfortable blanket ever lay across the bed. "Ahhhhh, warmth and comfort at last," Cindy sighed as she climbed beneath her gift. "This is amazing." The lovely blanket worked better than an IV pump of propofol as Cindy immediately began drifting off to sleep.

Chas stayed a little longer before heading home. Mission accomplished. His mom looked comfortable. "Mom, I'm gonna head back now," he said gently in Cindy's half-buried ear as he bent over to kiss her goodbye.

"This was the best gift ever, Chas," Cindy whispered halfway from her fall into a deep sleep. "Thank you so much."

"Absolutely," he affirmed, giving her a light parting squeeze.

I crawled onto the bed and lay beside my sweetheart for the first time in 17 days. And I went out like a light.

"Thanks so much for making the effort to come again, son," I said to Chas as he turned and gave me a not so gentle bear hug. "It's been quite the few weeks, and you guys have sacrificed so much for us."

"Don't even think of it, Dad. We love you guys, and no price is too great to pay to support you both in all this."

"Love you, son."

"Love you too, Dad." And with that, I walked my second-born son to the door.

I turned back to the bed with a heart full of gratitude for such amazing kids. I thought Cindy had drifted asleep so I rounded the window side of the bed to sit in the Lazy Boy style chair. But then I heard Cindy say something I couldn't quite make out. "What was that, honey?"

"Wanna try lying down beside me again?" Came the quiet yet hopeful request. "I don't think it's alarmed anymore."

I wasn't quite convinced, still on high alert for the alarms still sounding in my mind, but they suddenly dissipated as I remembered Chas' words, "No sacrifice is too great."

"I would love to," I agreed knowing she would find comfort in being close, another step forward in her slow but steady recovery.

I managed to get the rail down without setting off alarms. I crawled onto the bed and lay beside my sweetheart for the first time in 17 days. And I went out like a light.

| day 18
evaluations

I'm not sure if you enjoy roller coasters. I don't particularly care for them, and I especially don't like them in the hospital. The thrill of a real roller coaster isn't the ascent to the top; it's the free fall to the bottom. Hair and arms flying in the air. Lips flapping in the wind from the speed generated by the gravitational pull to earth. Screams accelerated by lungs filled with thrill and fear. But hospital roller coasters are the opposite; the thrills only come on ascent or progress. Fear falls without companion on descent. This morning I arrived feeling as if we were on a descent. Cindy was evidently uncomfortable, and it was bothersome.

But just as anxiety started gnawing at my heart, the PT guy showed up for a full evaluation. I didn't know it then, but the roller coaster was about to ascend.

"How's everyone doing today?" the football-player-sized guy asked.

"Well, to be honest, it looks as if the day is starting a little rough," I replied, looking back at Cindy with concern on my brow.

"Oh, that's not good to hear. Would you prefer I come back another time?"

"No, no," I was quick to answer. "Getting up and moving always helps."

The fit young man went to the bedside, double checking his chart, making sure he had her right name as he did so, "Hey, Cynthia. My name is John and I'm with physiotherapy. Would you be okay going through a short evaluation with me?"

"I suppose that'd be okay," Cindy responded in tired agreement.

"Okay, how about I help you sit up, and we'll begin really easy like," the therapist proceeded as he gently helped Cindy sit up, showing his expertise in how to handle patients with care and support.

"Let's go ahead and start with some simple leg movement right here on the side of the bed," he instructed, having Cindy rotate her ankles and toes in different directions.

"Good job with those. Now I'll get the gait belt around you and we'll have you stand up and come over to the open space at the end of the bed."

I could already see that getting Cindy moving was doing her good.

"Okay, stand right here with your back to the wall. I'll lightly hold the belt while you walk forward to the door and backward to where we are standing now."

"That seems pretty simple," Cindy commented with confidence.

"Well, typically I work with older stroke patients, and you wouldn't believe how the simple things are the hardest to do. So that's why we start out easy. Something as easy as walking backward can be a real challenge," he explained.

Cindy went to the door and walked backward without a hitch.

"Okay, let's do some balance tests. Walk to the door again forward and backward, but this time I want you to stop every couple of steps and stand on one leg and count to three before proceeding."

Again, Cindy performed the task without an issue.

"Good job," the therapist complimented with a satisfied smile behind his mask. "Now I'm going to throw my pen on the floor, and I want you to go pick it up and bring it back to me."

He tossed his pen a few feet away and Cindy retrieved it without the slightest hesitation, manifesting good balance bending down, standing erect and turning back to present the pen to its owner.

The therapist took hold of his clipboard to look at Cindy's history again all the while nodding his head and mumbling to himself. "So you had a double subarachnoid hemorrhage just over two weeks ago," he stated, not actually asking either of us to confirm. "And you were in ICU 17 days total with only two days here in recovery," he added, still without addressing us directly. "I had expected to see some sort of challenge as simple as these little tests are, but I'm not seeing anything at all with balance or mobility."

"So that's a good thing, right?" I asked with eyes wide open.

"That's an amazing thing," he shot right back with glee. "I wasn't expecting to continue past this point, but let's go do the stairs." He grabbed Cindy's oxygen tank, transferred the line and had us head to the door. "There's a set of stairs at the end of the hall we can go down to."

We made our way down the hall. Admittedly I was pretty nervous about the stairway wondering if Cindy would have the strength to do them. We went through the heavy exit door and stood at the 6th floor set of stairs leading to the 7th floor. It felt like Mount Everest.

"Ok, Cynthia, we're going to go up this flight of stairs then turn around at the top and come back down. Feel free to hold the rail as that is normal for anybody. I'll carry the oxygen tank and lightly hold the gait belt for you. If at any time you get dizzy or feel faint, just say so and we'll stop."

"Okay," Cindy nodded in agreement and began to ascend the stairs with her extra tall Sherpa carrying the gear.

She didn't set any speed records on her way up, but she also didn't break stride or need to stop.

When they reached the top, John asked gently, "Would you like to rest or make your way down?"

"I'm good to go down," she replied, and the pair descended at the same pace as when they went up. As they reached the 6th floor landing again, they showed no intention of stopping, so I opened the door and they kept right on cruising, all the way back to the room. John loosened the gait belt off Cindy, and she lay back down in bed knowing she had spent her tiny reserve of energy. And I was certain she knocked her evaluation out of the park.

As the therapist hooked the oxygen hose back into the wall port, he announced his assessment, "I don't think Cynthia needs intensive rehab." My eyes widened in surprise. I felt the jerk of the hospital roller coaster as the thrill of ascent began.

"She is clearly functioning well enough to be at home. Her range of motion, balance and heck, the performance on the stairs was impressive!" He complimented as he pulled off his gloves, tossing them in the trash bin by the sink. "I'll put in my report a recommendation that she could do some outpatient physio if she wants, but even that will just be a recommendation and only if you feel she needs the extra help. Do you have stairs in your home and an area outside to walk?"

"We sure do," I quickly answered.

"Great, well this assessment has been a thrill for me. I work mostly with people who are seriously impaired, so today has been a definite bright spot seeing Cynthia's amazing recovery."

"Yeah, we are truly thankful," I agreed.

"Well, I've got one more patient to see down the hall, and after that, I'll write up Cynthia's report giving her an all clear from my end." And with that, the pleasant giant Sherpa gathered his clipboard and other gear and headed off to the next room.

I closed the door behind the therapist and then turned to Cindy, "Honey, can you believe that? No intensive rehab! You knocked it out of the park with every evaluation! And the stairs! You went up and down those like Rocky Balboa doing his daily workout!" I bent over to give her a congratulatory hug and squeeze.

"Yeah, I really was amazing, but now I'm heading to the canvas going out for the count," Cindy countered slowly as her voice trailed off to sleep. "I spent all I had for that performance, and it wasn't even very much."

I let the champ enjoy her rest as I could hardly contain myself with the outcome of the assessment. We cleared the last hurdle and were definitely on the final push. Of course, I didn't want to rush anything. I was totally willing to leave any decision about going home to the medical staff. In actuality, I figured we could be in recovery until the end of the week or even the beginning of the following week.

After lunch, Cindy received the first and only flowers of her stay in the hospital. It wasn't that friends and loved ones didn't care about her, but the ICU is no place for flowers and balloons. These flowers were especially meaningful, a perfect orchid arrangement from Kathy and her husband, Dan, former coworkers from our time in Papua New Guinea. Its elegant, lovely blooms reminded us of their special friendship. Kathy and Dan worked at a support center in Papua New Guinea with our organization. Any time we came out of the jungle on breaks, we would stay at their place. They had five kids. We had five kids. So, yes, all 14 of us would bunk out together. Their gift of orchids meant much to Cindy in many ways.

The neurology team arrived after lunch, along with the PA who had been working with Cindy all along. She was confident, assertive and very pregnant. Her soon-to-arrive child made her belly protrude through the confines of her lab coat.

"Are you ready to go home, Cindy?" the PA asked as she began the regimen of response questions and exercises identical to those of the past umpteen days.

"I was ready a week ago," Cindy stated emphatically yet seasoned with a look of gratitude.

The PA chuckled. "You've beaten all the odds, girl," she said." This has been an amazing recovery, and I know I can speak for the whole neurology team in saying that. It is a real thrill for us all when someone like yourself comes in with such a dire condition and then bounces back without any limitations."

"Well, I don't have much energy yet," Cindy countered.

"True and that energy will take time to build back, but you're headed toward that without any hang ups. I read the PT's evaluations, and he figures you're good to go without any intensive rehab. That's nearly unheard of with your condition."

"Well thank you for the great care and encouragement."

"Okay, I'll put the discharge orders in so you can go home in the morning!"

Discharge orders? Go home? No extensive rehab? Fully functioning recovery? The words hadn't sunk in...I was stunned. We were going home! We truly felt like the Israelites at the Red Sea these past few weeks hemmed in by impossibilities on every side. Only God Himself could overcome and deliver us from this trial. We needed miracles in a hurry, and they came. Cindy survived two powerful and scary brain hemorrhages. She nearly died twice, but God provided a miraculous escape. In her recovery, she had manifested zero neurological, physical or cognitive damage. And now, she required no intensive rehab. God had parted the sea. We were heading home on dry ground. The PA's words sounded like Handel's Messiah to me, and I played them over and over again in my head. Every crescendo gave praise and glory to God for going beyond all we could hope for.

> *God had parted the sea.* **We were heading home** *on dry ground.*

"Cindy will need a list of prescriptions to take home with her," the PA continued snapping me out of the concert of my mind. "We'll put in an order for delivery before you leave tomorrow."

"Sounds like a great plan," I responded with an exhausted breath of relief.

"Do either of you have any further questions before I head off to continue my rounds?"

I actually did have a question I couldn't resist asking, but in my years of experience, I had learned you shouldn't ever ask a woman if she's pregnant—never. But in this case, I half wondered if I would end up delivering the baby right there in Cindy's room, she was so great with child. So, I took the risk and said as she began to leave the room, "Yeah, I do have one more question."

"What would that be?"

"When's the baby due?" I asked with a smile to make our parting a little more personal and connected.

"A week to ten days, which is not soon enough," she chuckled.

"And is this your first?"

"Number four actually."

"Whoa!" I blurted out in surprise. "Well, you're not quite as crazy as we are. We had five."

"I'm pretty sure I'm crazy enough with four," her final response came as she slipped through the door marking the last time we'd see the neurology team paying a visit to our room.

I turned to Cindy like a little kid showing all the excitement of just being told he was headed to Disney World for Christmas vacation, "Honey, did you hear that? We're going home. Can you believe that? We've been discharged!"

I bent over Cindy and began to give her a hug as she lay beneath her super comfy blanket from Chas. "Yes, it's wonderful news," she responded in a slow voice. "Are you going to carry me all the way home? Cuz I don't think I could make it otherwise."

"Of course, I'll carry you the whole way! I wouldn't think otherwise," I joked.

"Then you've got yourself a deal," she replied as she trailed off to sleep.

| day 19
homeward bound

I arrived at the hospital with a skip in my step. It was my last visit of our nearly three-week stay. I was sure to greet the valets on the way through the front door and let them know the good news of our discharge. At the check-in counter, I made a bit of a humorous scene announcing it was my last visiting badge paying extra attention to making sure it was slapped on my chest right side up. What a difference it was to enter the hospital knowing it was your last day.

Maea arrived shortly after I did, with another homemade breakfast. We were giddy with conversation and thankfulness to God for actually going home.

At about 11:00 a.m., one of the RNs came to the room with the official discharge announcement. She left us with a stack of information, booklets on care, types of medications and how to recognize the symptoms of a stroke. Before leaving with a smile, the gal said we could leave after lunch once the prescriptions were delivered.

We ordered up our last lunch of amazing hospital cuisine while we waited for the pharmacy person to show up. Again, the wait felt like leaving school, when time slows down in the face of so much anticipation. We were about to walk out of the hospital. It hardly felt possible.

I was an emotional wreck. So, after finishing lunch I just tried to keep busy by boxing up mementos of love from friends, family and, of course, the precious littles.

Finally, there was a light knock at the partly closed door. The pharmacy lady came in with an armful of papers and prescription bottles. "How exciting you are officially discharged," she exclaimed.

"You can say that again," I responded with a fake smile worried about the cost of the prescriptions from the hospital pharmacy. We rarely ever use medications, and if we ever do, we buy them at the cheapest place around, Walmart. Our insurance didn't cover prescriptions, thus my uneasiness of what was coming.

The pharmacist finished explaining the different prescriptions and then asked, "Would you like to pay cash or by credit card."

Thinking I'd rather not pay at all, I produced my credit card from my pocket wincing on the inside and bracing myself for the pain of what was coming.

The gal took the card with a "thank you" and then pulled out a mobile card reader for the transaction. "That'll be $29.47," she nonchalantly said while inserting the chip end of the card into the reader.

"Did I just hear her right," I asked myself. "Did she leave off a couple of numbers before the decimal point?"

Just to clarify, I asked, "How much did you say?"

"Just $29.47," came the clarification with an "I bet you weren't expecting that" kind of a smile.

"But didn't you leave off a couple of numbers before the decimal, like a one and zero?"

"Nope. We found a way to make it down to $29.47."

I couldn't believe what I just heard. *Wow, that's one of the foothills at the Red Sea, God has already removed,* I thought to myself.

The pleasant lady handed me the receipt from the credit card machine and then was on her way to her next delivery. I turned to tell Cindy what just happened, but she had dozed off beneath her favorite blanket.

I took advantage of the time to shuttle boxes and bags of mementos to the car in preparation for leaving. On my way, I stopped at the nurses' station. Several nurses were working away at computers, one of whom was assigned to Cindy's room. I went up to her quietly and said, "Hey, may I ask a favor?"

"Absolutely. Whatever you need," she replied, looking away from her work without skipping a beat.

"I'm just carting some of our keepsakes down to the car while my wife Cindy is resting," I began.

"Would you like me to get an aide and a wheelchair ready? How exciting you get to go home," she interjected.

"Thank you, but not quite yet," I responded. "I'm just going to let her rest before we take off, but my favor is a little different from that."

"Sure, what do you need?"

I worked hard to hold back the tears as I looked down into the box I was holding. "Please make sure no one cuts off the DNR bracelet," I began struggling to finish my request. "I would like to do that."

"Absolutely, Mr. Wall," she came back in total understanding. "That will be a very special moment, and I'll personally make sure none of us does that."

"Yeah, it'll be very special indeed after all we've been through. Thanks." And I turned before my quivering lip got too far out of control and headed to the elevators.

After a second trip to the car, I grabbed a pair of hospital scissors a nurse had left by the sink in the room and pulled a chair over beside my sleeping beauty. I refrained from waking her and enjoyed a time of just thanking God once again for all He had done. I still couldn't believe, as I sat there looking at my dear wife enjoying her peaceful sleep, we were able to go home. Before long she woke with only a slight smile as her tired mind and body remembered that she was being discharged.

"Hey, honey. Are you ready to head home?" I asked softly, giving her time to wake up fully.

"Yeah, I think so. What time is it?" she asked with a yawn and slight stretch of her arm before tucking it back in under the comfort of her blanket.

"Just before two o'clock."

"How long have I been sleeping?"

"Oh, I'd say at least an hour and a half or so," I estimated.

"Well, if we are able to leave, then I guess I better get moving. It's just so comfortable under this cozy blanket," she said with a sigh of satisfaction.

"There is one more thing we need to do before leaving," I said, taking Cindy's arm out from under her blanket.

"What's that?"

I showed Cindy the purple bracelet on her wrist with the letters "DNR" printed in bold white. "Honey," I began as my lips quivered and my eyes teared. "Do you know what this stands for?"

She crinkled her brow in concentration and softly said the letters, "D-N-R." She paused for a moment and looked up at me with an unsure look. "Department of Natural Resources?"

I chuckled as I wondered if that would be her first guess. "No, it doesn't mean Department of Natural Resources even though your legs could pass as a state forest after 19 days without a razor." That got my favorite eye roll and cornered smile.

I'm not sure how the actual acronym even got out of my mouth, but I continued, "It means Do Not Resuscitate." Tears streamed down my face as I tried to continue.

"I'm OK you put it on me," Cindy assured me with eyes full of love and understanding.

I couldn't talk. I gently supported her arm with my hand then slipped the hospital scissors under the band and said, "Honey, God gives, He takes and now He has given again." And I snipped the code releasing her from any weight its meaning had carried. I began weeping uncontrollably so Cindy reached out with the now unshackled arm and tenderly pulled me toward her, cradling my head on the side of her neck where I continued to sob.

> God gives, he takes and now he has given again.

After a measure of unmarked time, I lifted my tear-soaked face, apologizing for my runny nose and tears.

"It's OK, honey," she assured me with all sincerity. But the sincerity at the perfect moment turned to panic. "But you better get me to the bathroom right now!"

We both had a laugh through tears of thankfulness and gratitude for all God had done as we were homeward bound.

| epilogue

Our return home on dry ground to recovery has taken time. Cindy's fatigue initially was heavy and overwhelming. But her drive to build her strength back up was measurable with daily walks and long rests. At first, our walks went only as far as her brother's driveway part of the way down the lane we share. But as her strength came back, she was able to make new goals of getting all the way to the mailbox and then all the way to the intersecting road at the end of our township road. After about four months, Cindy is up to walking two miles a day, and she has returned to taking on her regular tasks around the house once again. We have had several follow-up appointments, and the doctors are simply amazed at the recovery she has had without any residual effects of her two aneurysms. Dr. S has been so impressed, he has asked Cindy to join him in one of his university lectures as an exemplary case in recovering from a subarachnoid hemorrhage.

You will remember my writing about being at the "Red Sea," hemmed in on every side by impossibilities from which only God could deliver us. There were the aneurysms chasing us like Pharaoh's army. And there was the sea of unknown recovery before us. Well, God miraculously took care of those, but what about the mountains that were impossible to get over, blocking any way of escape? The mountains were the financial burden that quickly piled up in diluvian force and measure before our very eyes. We had an insurance plan to cover some expenses, but it wasn't extensive in its reach. It wasn't hard to figure the enormity of critical care cost when you throw in an ambulance, airlift, 17 days in ICU and multiple follow-up visits. We were looking at hundreds of thousands of dollars in medical bills.

During our years of work as missionaries, I fully embraced the challenge of truly looking to God to meet our needs; I mean truly trusting God and not asking people for money. After all, we believed God had led us into mission work; therefore we were going to ask only Him to provide. Back in the day, they called raising support deputation or the "street term," the tin cup tour. Basically, it involved traveling around to friends and churches earnestly seeking prayer support…and money.

As a couple, we resolved never to ask a person for one red cent. And we didn't, except one time, and I regret it to this day. When we lived in the jungle, we began an airstrip project and needed a tractor for the construction of the 70x600 yard piece of ground that would become our supply link. Well, I put out a newsletter asking for people to get involved by contributing to a tractor fund. As soon as the letter left my hands, God smote my heart with guilt for not trusting Him. We ended up with one donation of $100. I vowed after that lesson not to look to man to provide for my needs again. We did end up getting a tractor, and thankfully our coworker had a farming background and was able to salvage an old Massey Ferguson 165 that was in a million pieces.

So here we were, no longer missionaries doing God's work in a land far off, but unemployed mid-50-year olds looking at a stack of medical bills we had no way of taking care of. What were we to do? Have spaghetti dinner fundraisers? Start a GoFundMe page? Ask relatives or rich friends to help?

No, I resolved I would tell no one about the amount we needed and the fact that our insurance would fall way short. So, I rested. If God could deliver us from Pharaoh and bring us home on dry ground, he could move the mountains. And he did. No more aneurysms, no residual physical effects in recovery and no overhanging medical bills. We are free on all sides. Simply amazing.

So what about the other thing I mentioned at the beginning of this journey. How do you look at your life? Do you have a win-win mentality? If you faced the crisis of your lifetime, what would your response be? I don't think anyone can honestly answer that question. But I do know what you can do to prepare for it. Cindy and I are not special people. We are normal everyday people who live a pretty boring life. But before God, we understand who we are and what God has done for us through His Son's work on our behalf. With that understanding, we live a win-win life. We D-N-R, because it's God's job.

| acknowledgments

First of all I would like to acknowledge our family, both immediate and extended, near and far. Your support of love, prayers, meals, and many other things were so much appreciated. Cindy's medical team was hugely impressed with the care you all provided in her recovery.

We have so many friends all around the world that we are also very thankful for. So many of you reached out with care that was beyond the call of duty. Whether you reached out from within the USA, Canada, Australia, Europe, Asia or South America, you are all appreciated.

Special mention needs to be made for the editing help that Cindy Serratore and Ruth Peterson provided for the writing of this book. Thanks for doing the hard yards with me and getting the manuscript to print quality.

I would also like to thank and acknowledge the emergency services of Beltrami County, Bemidji Ambulance, and Sanford Health. You all played a vital part in listening, responding, and treating on our day of days. Thank you seems too small, but I'd like to make it big for you all.

| upcoming books
by Dave Wall

At What Expense – Stepping In

A Tribe's Journey from Cannibalism to Meeting the Outside World

At What Expense – Stepping Out

A Tribe's Journey from the Rain Forest to the Plantation

At What Expense – Invited In

A Tribe's Journey Inviting a White Man to Live Among Them

Seeds from the Jungle

A collection of short stories that will bring nourishment to your soul.

| about the author

Dave Wall spent the majority of his
adult working career as a linguist,
consultant, and director with a mission
agency near the equator in the South
Pacific. Life wasn't always easy for
Dave and his family as they lived for 20
years in remote conditions with little
direct access to medical care and the
conveniences of the modern world. But
the life experience gained from learning
several languages and immersion in

bizarre tribal culture has equipped Dave to relate life experience in a front
row seat kind of way. He has used his skills in language and communication
to take you deep inside the most challenging experience of his life in
DNR - Do Not Resuscitate. Dave and his wife Cindy currently reside by a
lake in northern Minnesota and continue to enjoy their five children and 11
grandchildren. And of course, Dave still plays hockey.

CPSIA information can be obtained
at www.ICGtesting.com
Printed in the USA
LVHW051931190921
698209LV00010B/1351